MICHAEL JACKSON REWIND

MICHAEL JACKSON REWIND

THE LIFE & LEGACY OF POP MUSIC'S KING

DARYL EASLEA

FOREWORD BY NDUGU CHANCLER

Race Point
PUBLISHING

Quarto is the authority on a wide range of topics.

Quarto educates, entertains and enriches the lives of
our readers—enthusiasts and lovers of hands-on living.

www.quartoknows.com

Please see page 214 for photography credits.

Back cover quote: Jackson, Michael, and Bryan Monroe. "Michael Jackson in His Own Words," Ebony magazine, Vol. 63, No. 2, December 2007.

First published in the United States of America in 2016 by
Race Point Publishing, a member of
Quarto Publishing Group USA Inc.
142 West 36th Street, 4th Floor
New York, New York 10018

www.quartoknows.com

10 9 8 7 6 5 4 3 2 1

ISBN: 978-1-63106-253-7

Names: Easlea, Daryl, author.
Title: Michael Jackson, rewind : the life and legacy of pop music's king /
   Daryl Easlea.
Description: New York : Race Point Publishing, 2016. | Includes
   bibliographical references and index.
Identifiers: LCCN 2016027229 | ISBN 9781631062537 (hardcover)
Subjects: LCSH: Jackson, Michael, 1958-2009. | Rock musicians--United
   States--Biography.
Classification: LCC ML420.J175 E27 2016 | DDC 782.42166092 [B] --dc23 LC record available at https://lccn.loc.gov/2016027229

Editorial Director: Jeannine Dillon
Project Editor: Erin Canning
Art Director: Merideth Harte
Cover Art: © Seanings
Cover Design: Phil Buchanan
Book Design: Renato Stanisic

Printed in China

CONTENTS

"AN INNER FEELING THAT A PROJECT IS SPECIAL": MICHAEL JACKSON

BY NDUGU CHANCLER

From the 1970s through the 1990s, music was developing a variety of personalities. This variety was compounded by the many innovations that were being created in electronic instruments and recording techniques. Jazz embraced electronic instruments and utilized rock and R&B sounds and rhythms. Jazz musicians, like myself, who were the backbone of session players, were making these adjustments in concepts, approach, sound, instruments, and attitudes. These innovations opened the door for artists to shape and develop new directions in music across jazz, pop, rock, and R&B.

Recording techniques allowed creative individuals more latitude because of the expansion of recording tracks available, alongside the creation of new outboard gear for sound enhancement. The combination of technology and the openness of artists and players meant new recording styles and musical sounds were being created across genres. Breakout recordings affected the sound of music going into the '80s and '90s. Artists such as Miles Davis, Stevie Wonder, Herbie Hancock, Jimi Hendrix, the Beatles, Blood Sweat and Tears, Prince, to name a few, had all pushed the envelope, creating new directions in the music.

We were all affected by these sounds and innovations. With the technology came new recording techniques. These new techniques incorporated using live instruments along with synthesizers and drum machines. This new technology made it possible for songwriters to finish more complete demos in their home studios. Some of these demos actually became the final recording or utilized some of the parts from the demos.

OPPOSITE: *"Michael Jackson was the consummate professional." —Ndugu Chancler, 2016.*

Coming out of the shadows of jazz, fusion, Latin rock, and funk, the transition for me to the studio as a session player embracing the new technology and musical concepts was one I welcomed. After having been a part of the Miles Davis, Herbie Hancock, George Duke, and Santana bands, the recording studio became home for me. Living in Los Angeles, which at that time was one of the recording centers, I began to be called by many of the top-of-the-line artists, producers, and arrangers. During the '70s and '80s, I began to get session calls from Lionel Richie, Kenny Rogers, the Crusaders, Chuck Jackson, and Quincy Jones. Quincy Jones, like Miles Davis, was always ahead of the curve while remaining relevant and contemporary.

Many artists broke away from their respective groups to create their own individual identity and sound during this period. The true genius of these artists started to shine away from the groups they were in. One of the most prolific artists to emerge from a popular group was Michael Jackson. The rise to individual superstardom for Michael slowly manifested itself on his solo recordings and collaborations with other solo artists. To achieve this steep rise to superstardom, a winning team had to be assembled and learn to work in sync with each other. Having already been a star working with the Jacksons, Michael would have to generate his own sound and identity separate from what he had already created with his brothers.

Michael Jackson found his winning team in producer Quincy Jones and engineer Bruce Swedien. With Michael exercising his own songwriting abilities, along with Quincy

assembling the right musicians to record each song, the stage was set. Bruce Swedien would be the innovative engineer to capture all of the magic to tape (there was no Pro Tools back then!). The launching pad was set with the release of *Off the Wall*. With this winning team plus the addition of another breakaway songwriter, Rod Temperton (formerly of the group Heatwave), *Off the Wall* set up a new identity for and the recognition of a new sound coming from him. *Off the Wall* featured an all-star cast of stellar musicians and broke sales records at that time.

Off the Wall set the stage for *Thriller*. The concept behind *Off the Wall* was great songs and great music. The concept behind *Thriller* was great songs that could each stand alone and be great like classic snapshots. Michael brought in songs with new concepts. Quincy once again assembled a handpicked team for each song. Bruce stretched his recording techniques to the limit by using multiple multitrack tape machines and SMPTE time code to aid in tape sequencing.

After having worked with Quincy and Bruce on other projects, I was totally elated to get the call to work with Quincy, Bruce, and Michael. I had known some of the other Jacksons from playing in a celebrity softball league, but I had not spent a lot of time around Michael. Michael and Rod trusted me and were convinced by Quincy that I was the right drummer to marry live drums with the drum machine on *Thriller*. In the studio, all of the songs felt special and had a distinct uniqueness to them. With Michael and Quincy explaining the inspiration behind each song, it was easy to feel the vibe and concept for each one. There was an underlying magical feeling in each song that pulled something deeper than normal out of you.

During the recording, each song felt special. It was hard to know which song was going to be "the one." "Billie Jean" was unique in that the track starts with this hypnotic drum groove, while "Baby Be Mine" had this new vocal approach from Michael that was airy and gritty at the same time. Each track brought out different characteristics of Michael's vocal stylings.

Often in your work, you have an inner feeling that a project is special. We all felt that *Thriller* was special. In the studio, we imagined how nice it would be to sell three million units more than *Off the Wall* . . . the rest is history!

Thriller and *Bad* differ in that *Bad* utilized even more of the electronic technology that was now available. The only live band track on *Bad* was "I Can't Stop Loving You," which we did with Michael and the other musicians all live in the studio. By the time *Bad* was done, technology had advanced and Michael, Quincy, and Bruce were ahead of the pack in utilizing it. These recordings created new standards for recording and were the basis for many of the components of Pro Tools, Logic, and other digital recording software.

By this time, Michael Jackson had been crowned undeniably the King of Pop. The genius of Michael Jackson was now proven, both on recordings and in live performance. Michael's albums broke new ground musically, technically, and sonically. As great work stands the test of time, these great works hold up against the music of yesterday, today, and tomorrow.

Michael Jackson was the consummate professional. He worked hard. He knew what he wanted, and knew who to go to to get it. The genius of Michael was that he had musical layers as a performer and a songwriter. He had high musical standards and strived to achieve them all of the time. Michael Jackson has left a recording and performance legacy duplicated by no one, imitated by many.

His great works stand the test of time and hold their own.

The legacy lives on.

Among his work on *Thriller* and *Bad*, **Ndugu Chancler** provided one of the most famous drumbeats of all-time on "Billie Jean." He has also played with artists such as Frank Sinatra, Miles Davis, George Duke, Weather Report, Santana, and Lionel Richie. He played on "Love Is in Control (Finger on the Trigger)" by Donna Summer. Listed as one of the top twenty-five drummers in the world, aside from his ongoing musical career, he is currently professor of jazz and contemporary music studies at the Thornton School of Music, University of Southern California.

WHERE DID WE GO WRONG?

JUNE 25, 2009

"The world is in shock but somehow he knew exactly how his fate would be played out some day more than anyone else knew, and he was right."

—LISA MARIE PRESLEY, 2009[1]

"Maybe now, Michael, they will leave you alone."

—MARLON JACKSON, JULY 7, 2009[2]

Michael Joseph Jackson—the King of Pop, the maker of the world's biggest-selling album, and a man who had been in showbusiness for more or less all of his fifty years—was pronounced dead at 2:26 p.m. Pacific Time on Thursday, June 25, 2009. He had been taken to Ronald Reagan UCLA Medical Center on Westwood Plaza in Los Angeles after being found unconscious at his 100 North Carolwood Drive home in the Holmby Hills just over two hours previously. Jackson had been attended to by his physician, Dr. Conrad Murray, who had administered Propofol, among other drugs, for Jackson's insomnia, as he was preparing for a string of comeback concerts.

The portentous news began to spread like wildfire. It started with rumors emanating immediately from the Ronald Reagan UCLA Medical Center, and intensified as Jackson's mother, Katherine; his children Prince, Paris, and Blanket; and his brother Jermaine arrived. Showbiz gossip site TMZ.com reported that Jackson had been taken to the hospital. Initially other sources were cautious of taking the website's word as gospel; soon, the site announced

OPPOSITE: *The King of Pop in silhouette.*

Jackson's passing, ahead of the official statement.

It was time to go public. Michael's brother Jermaine was appointed the Jackson family spokesperson and faced the world's media; he told the awaiting throng, "This is hard. My brother, the legendary King of Pop, passed away on Thursday, June 25, 2009, at 2:26 p.m. It is believed he suffered cardiac arrest." He explained that Jackson's personal physician had been with him at the house and had tried to resuscitate him. He said that the paramedics had also tried to revive his brother, and that, "upon arriving at the hospital at 1:14 p.m., a team of doctors, including emergency physicians and a cardiologist, worked

to resuscitate him for a period of more than one hour, but were unsuccessful." After confirming that a full autopsy would soon be carried out, Jermaine concluded, "May Allah be with you, Michael, always."

Fans immediately began to congregate around the Medical Center; the Holmby Hills home; Neverland Ranch; the original Jackson family home in Gary, Indiana; the Hitsville studios in Detroit; the Apollo Theater in Harlem. It was as if no landmark associated with him would be overlooked in the tributes being paid. On June 27, the family issued a more formal statement, caught in the whirlwind of grief that had circled the

planet for Jackson's passing: "Our beloved son, brother, uncle, and father of three children has gone so unexpectedly, in such a tragic way and much too soon. It leaves us, his family, speechless and devastated to a point where communication with the outside world seems almost impossible at times." The subtle retreat into their private lives was dignified at the moment when the world stopped and went into a global grief that was not dissimilar to Princess Diana beforehand and David Bowie and Prince afterward.

The scale of Jackson's passing was marked by tributes from US president Barack Obama, Nelson Mandela, and UK prime minister Gordon Brown. The US House of Representatives observed a minute's silence. The testimonies of friends and fellow musicians tumbled out across the world's media. Beyoncé said, "The reason I am here is due

OPPOSITE: "May Allah be with you, Michael, always." —Jermaine Jackson, June 25, 2009. ABOVE: Jackson's mother, Katherine, being shown proposals for the tribute to Jackson in Gary, Indiana, 2009. BELOW LEFT: Tributes flood the front garden of the original Jackson family home. BELOW RIGHT: The "Jackson Family Blvd" street sign.

to Michael Jackson"; Robin Gibb, whose group, the Bee Gees, had its pop crown taken in the early '80s by Jackson, added, "This tragedy should teach us a lesson to value and praise those gifts while we still have them in the world."

As with all tragedies, whether of such magnitude or not, a family lost a father, a brother, an ex-husband. One of the most elegant, raw memorials came from Lisa Marie Presley, Jackson's wife in the '90s. She wrote on her MySpace page the following day about how her ex-husband knew that one day it would end like this. She, like many others, had tried to help him. "The person I failed to help is being transferred right now to the LA County coroner's office for his autopsy. All of my indifference and detachment that I worked so hard to achieve over the years has just gone into the bowels of hell and right now I am gutted." She later told Oprah Winfrey, "I was in England; it was the strangest day of my life. I was crying all day." John Travolta texted messages of support to Presley in her "real honest-to-goodness shock; I was floored."[3] There were many raw emotions on display, but there was an overriding feeling from many that something could and should have been done to help someone who slipped away in front of everyone's very eyes.

THE MEMORIAL SERVICE

After a private family ceremony, held on July 7, there was a public memorial service at the Staples Center in Los Angeles. Promoters AEG gave away 17,500 free tickets through an online lottery. More than 1.2 million people applied for the places in little over twenty-four hours. Ironically, this was the venue where Jackson had been rehearsing his *This Is It* concerts. He returned to the stage in a blue-velvet-lined, solid bronze coffin plated with 14-carat gold.

There were speeches by the Rev. Al Sharpton and actress and one-time Jackson paramour Brooke Shields ("Michael saw everything with his heart"); Smokey Robinson read messages from Diana Ross and Nelson Mandela; Motown founder Berry Gordy gave an emotional address; Queen Latifah read out an especially moving poem by Maya Angelou entitled "We Had Him." Lionel Richie, Stevie Wonder, Mariah Carey, and Usher

all performed. Jermaine Jackson sang Charlie Chaplin's "Smile," one of Michael's very favorite songs. One of the most moving moments was when Michael's eleven-year-old daughter, Paris, falteringly told the packed arena, "I just wanted to say, ever since I was born, daddy has been the best father you could ever imagine. And I just wanted to say I love him so much."

In September of that year, Madonna, very much the Queen to his King of Pop, offered an eloquent eulogy to Jackson at the MTV Video Music Awards in New York. "When Michael Jackson was six, he became a superstar, and was perhaps the world's most beloved child," she said. "When I was six, my mother died. I think he got the shorter end of the stick. I never had a mother, but he never had a childhood. And when you never get to have something, you become obsessed by it. I spent my childhood searching for my mother figures. Sometimes I was successful,

KING OF POP

MICHAEL J. JACKSON

AUGUST 29, 1958

JUNE 25, 2009

HOME TOWN OF MICHAEL JACKSON—GARY, IN.

"Never can say good bye"

but how do you re-create your childhood when you are under the magnifying glass of the world?"[4] His endless attempts to re-create his lost childhood had proved the double-edged sword that had brought him such unparalleled success and, ultimately, such fathomless misery.

The formalities of death and the resulting inquests had to be dealt with. On February 8, 2010, an inquest proved that negligence and over-dosage of Propofol, a surgical anesthetic known as "the milk of amnesia," had killed the pop legend. The trial of Conrad Murray (People of the State of California v. Conrad Robert Murray) began on September 27, 2011, at Los Angeles County Superior Court. After a twenty-four-day trial, Murray was found guilty of involuntary manslaughter.

Like Elvis Presley and John Lennon before

him, everybody wanted a piece of Michael Jackson now that he was no longer here. The only person who could sully the Jackson myth was Jackson himself; now his rehabilitation could begin. He once again became the hottest pop star on the planet.

Within a year, with sales going through the roof and demand for Jackson-related products sky-high, a new contract would be negotiated with Sony to release previously unheard material. The debts that Jackson had accrued so heavily in his later years would soon be eradicated, because there was now no one frittering away the revenue with ostentatious largesse.

The Jackson family ended its July 27 statement with the phrase "carry on, so his legacy will live forever." Carrying on was *exactly* what was going to happen. His position was unassailable. The King of Pop was dead. Long Live the King.

OPPOSITE: *Queen Latifah speaking at Jackson's memorial service, July 7, 2009.* ABOVE: *The monument to Jackson on the lawn of the family's former home in Gary, Indiana.* BELOW: *"I just wanted to say I love him so much." —Paris Jackson at the memorial service.*

KING OF POP

The final eighteen months of Michael Jackson's life were exceptionally busy. As he crisscrossed the globe, he had to reestablish himself as the King of Pop. His most recent recordings were ebbing further and further into his history. Jackson had never gone so long without releasing a new album. By spring 2009, the most audacious plan was unveiled to put the luster back to make this superstar shine: a series of dates at London's O2 Arena, one of the world's most prestigious venues.

CHAPTER 1

YOU'VE SEEN MY FACE BEFORE

THIS IS IT. . .

Q: Do you think you'll be doing this at eighty?

A: The truth is, umm, no. Not the way James Brown did, or Jackie Wilson did, where they just ran it out, they killed themselves. In my opinion, I wish [Brown] could have slowed down and been more relaxed and enjoyed his hard work.[1]

Michael Jackson released his best album ever in early 2008. The problem was, he'd already released it before, two and a half decades earlier. Issued globally on February 11, *Thriller 25* is a CD/DVD set that thoroughly celebrates the most successful album of all time. It also offers a modicum of pizzazz with reworked, remixed versions of his classics adding contemporary chart stars to the tracks as well as including another unreleased song from the sessions. Whereas Michael Sembello's "Carousel" had made it to the 2001 Special Edition of *Thriller*, this time the Steve Porcaro and Michael Sherwood–written "For All Time" was the song selected from the archive as the previously unheard track.

Thriller 25 is also notable in that something finally emerged from the ongoing will.i.am/Michael Jackson collaborations that had begun during Jackson's sojourn in Ireland back in 2006. *Thriller 25* contains three extensive overhauls and mixes that the Black Eyed Peas leader did for "P.Y.T.," "The Girl Is Mine," and "Beat It." Adding a layer of insistent electronics to Quincy Jones' original production, all have additional raps by the performer/producer born William Adams. By far the most successful is "The Girl Is Mine 2008," which,

OPPOSITE: *"When I say this is it, I really mean this is it." —Jackson announces his string of concerts, March 2009.*

Michael Jackson collaborators Akon and will.i.am, 2008.

by using an early demo version, removes Paul McCartney's vocal altogether, leaving just Jackson singing before a convincing will.i.am flow. Reflecting just how white hot the group was in 2007/2008, fellow Black Eyed Pea Fergie contributes vocals to the mix of "Beat It."

Twenty-first-century phenomenon Aliaume Damala Badara Akon Thiam, better known as Akon, produced and co-wrote a new version of "Wanna Be Startin' Somethin' " that actually adds to the original by stripping it down and playing it differently initially, with a new verse sung over a lone piano. Elsewhere, Kanye West gives "Billie Jean" a contemporary twist. It's not a patch on

the original, but it does skillfully allow Jackson an air of the cutting edge, with West then on his way to becoming one of the most influential rappers of his generation.

What made *Thriller 25* doubly appealing was that the double-disc set finally brought together the promos—or, as Jackson liked to say, "short films"—made for "Billie Jean," "Beat It," and "Thriller" into one place, alongside Jackson's groundbreaking performance of "Billie Jean" on *Motown 25: Yesterday, Today, and Forever* in 1983.

The hardback book edition, with its gold embossing and front cover still of Jackson in his pre-zombie transformation glory, from the "Thriller" video, is a bold reassertion of Jackson: how he was and how, for many people forever wanted to see him. Sony put all of its marketing might behind the release; the label launched a forty-episode "Thrillercast" podcast, with artists such as Chris Brown and KRS-One talking about the influence the album had on them. Global variants were made, and the ever-loyal Japanese market was rewarded with the super-rare session outtake "Got the Hots."

Thriller 25 was an enormous commercial success given that it was fundamentally a repackage, selling three million copies worldwide in twelve weeks and reaching the Top 10 in many of Jackson's traditional strongholds. It hit No. 3 in the UK and topped the US Catalog chart. This proved to Jackson that there was a huge audience for his work—albeit in a far more straightforward form than some of his recent (if now rather distant) releases. Soon after this release, as if to underline its importance, *Thriller* was identified as a work of great cultural significance when it was brought into the Library of Congress in May. Michael Jackson still had a great many admirers, even at the highest level.

NEVER NEVERLAND?

Whole books have been written about the financial complexities of Michael Jackson's life during his final months. Suffice it to say, by now, he was not in rude health financially; he needed a lifeline, and there were a great many people circling nearby to offer it to him. A recurring rumor was that he would play a string of dates at London's prestigious O2 Arena in partnership with the Anschutz Entertainment Group (AEG), which would go some way to canceling his debt.

It was reported in February 2008 that Jackson's beloved yet troubled home, the Neverland Ranch, would be auctioned off in March unless he paid the $24 million he owed for the upkeep of the property. By May, the investment company Colony Capital LLC had stepped in and purchased the loan Jackson had himself financed with Fortress Investment Group to save the house. Colony Capital was owned by billionaire Tom Barrack. Jackson said, "I am pleased with recent developments involving Neverland Ranch and I am in discussions with Colony and Tom Barrack with regard to the Ranch and other matters that would allow me to focus on the future."[2] The house and its part of his legend was, for the time being, safe. However, Jackson had had little interest in living there since the Arvizo scandal and subsequent lawsuit.

Michael Jackson turned fifty on August 29, 2008. To celebrate, Sony released another compilation. *King of Pop* was one of the first releases to fully utilize the power of social media by engaging global fan bases to each select their own variants on the track listing from a pool of one hundred tracks; only "Billie Jean" is on every version. Released in twenty-eight different editions (including versions for India, China, and the Philippines), the album hit No. 1 around the world and fared well on import in the United States, where it was not issued domestically. Again, this underlined the fact that there was a great desire to reclaim Jackson's legend rather than the reality of his final years.

At the end of 2008, with discussion already underway between AEG and Jackson's current manager Tohme Tohme (who had begun representing Jackson in mid-2008), a company entitled AllGood Entertainment Inc, led by Patrick Allocco in association with Michael's father, Joe Jackson, signed an agreement with Jackson's old manager, Frank DiLeo, who had informed Allocco that he would represent Jackson in order for there to be a Jacksons reunion tour. This was categorically denied by Jackson and quickly put on ice. Another ghost of the recent past was exorcised when an amicable settlement was reached out of court in a lawsuit that had been filed by Sheik Abdulla Hamad Al-Khalifa.

THE DOME PROJECT

Although the fans' appetite for Jackson to return to concert performance was simply huge, he was not overly interested in doing so. Asked about touring by *Ebony* magazine in 2007, he said, "I don't care about long tours. But what I love about touring is that it sharpens one's craft beautifully. That's what I love about Broadway, that's why actors turn to Broadway, to sharpen their skills . . . it takes years to become a great entertainer.

Years. You can't just grab some guy out of obscurity and throw 'em out there and expect for this person to compete with that person. It'll never work. And the audience knows it; they can see it. The way they gesture their hand, move their body, the way they do anything with the microphone, or the way they bow. They can see it right away."[3] Perhaps there was a way to give Jackson his own Broadway show, albeit on a much larger scale.

A deal was done with AEG Live: Jackson would play a series of ten dates at the O2 Arena on the banks of the River Thames in London in July, with the possibility of adding more if demand was sufficient. (The O2 Arena had started life as the ill-fated "Millennium Dome": a yearlong exhibition to introduce the new century. It was doomed to failure as, rather than a huge interactive theme park, it seemed all too much like a worthy school lesson.) The working title for the concerts was to be "the Dome Project."

The president and chief executive of AEG, Randy Phillips, was later to announce to the media that the first ten dates alone would earn the singer approximately £50 million. Although Jackson was not overly keen, he knew that doing the shows would go some way to redressing the balance of the debt that he had been accruing as the twenty-first century continued.

It was time for Jackson to return to what he needed to do. As Nelson George writes, "Between 2002 and 2009, he released no new music. Between the domestic backlash, arguments with his record label, and his own indulgent production process (and lifestyle), a man once so consumed with work stopped doing what he had been born to do."[4] It was, in one sense,

a simple way to deal with it all: go back to work for one last time—that was, after all, how he was programmed—and make such a song and dance of it that the whole world would know. Whereas in America people had grown somewhat tired of Jackson, in the UK there was still an enormous thirst for him and his work, even with all the considerable ups and downs that the artist and his audience had been through.

As part of the deal, Jackson would move to a $38 million house on 100 North Carolwood Drive in the Holmby Hills area of Los Angeles, a short distance from the Staples Center, the 18,000-capacity sports and concert venue at 1111 S. Figueroa St., Los Angeles, about a thirty-minute drive away. Designed in 2002 by local architect Richard Landry, the house had once been owned

OPPOSITE: *One of the twenty-eight editions of the* King of Pop *album.* TOP: *Michael Jackson with Mohamed Hadid and family, November 2007.* ABOVE: *The O2 Arena, Greenwich Peninsula, London.*

by Sean Connery. It was reported that the rent was $100,000 a month; AEG was picking up the tab. In consideration of his stamina, it was stipulated that he not be onstage for stretches of longer than thirteen minutes at a time during the two-hour show.

THIS IS IT

By the time Jackson and AEG were ready to go public, the show had been retitled *This Is It*. On Saturday, March 5, 2009, Michael Jackson appeared at the Grand Concourse at the O2 Arena on London's Greenwich Peninsula to announce his forthcoming shows.

After arriving ninety minutes late, Jackson was introduced by British TV personality Dermot O'Leary. Then, in front of 7,000 fans and 350 reporters from around the world, he finally emerged after a further ninety-second delay. Standing in front of a backdrop of vivid red curtains, he mumbled and giggled his way though his prepared announcement, which he punctuated by throwing V-signs at his adoring audience. He was back in front of the world's lenses for the right reasons, and he was enjoying it, even if he seemed slightly bemused by the whole operation.

Jackson spoke falteringly, as if English was his second language. "Thank you all," he exclaimed. "This is it. I just want to say these will be my final shows, performances in London. This will be it. When I say this is it, I really mean this is it." He broke off the speech to laugh and murmur something to O'Leary, and then, quite overawed by the fans' chanting, patted his heart and opened his arms wide. He continued, "I'll be performing the songs my fans want to hear. This is the final curtain call, okay, and I'll see you in July. I love you. I really do. You have to know that. I love you so much, really, from the bottom of my heart. This is it, and see you in July." In retrospect, the speech almost feels like a goodbye note.

AEG issued a statement straight away to say that "Michael Jackson has not played a series of concerts since he last toured twelve years ago. These dramatic shows promise an explosive return with a band of the highest caliber, a state-of-the-art stage show, and an incredible surprise support act."

On the evening of Sunday, March 8, 2009, at 9:30 p.m., during a commercial break in the finale of the celebrity competition show *Dancing on Ice*, a three-and-a-half-minute advertisement for the concerts was screened in the UK on ITV—the only time a musical artist had taken over an entire break. With a marketing barrage like few had seen before, the shows went on sale on March 13, with an elaborate pre-sale and registration process. The shows were originally due to begin on July 8, although that date was subsequently put back to July 13 as a result of production delays. At one point, Jackson's website was experiencing 16,000 hits a second. In two hours, all 190,000 tickets were sold. An amazing forty additional dates were added in blocks going through to March 10, 2010. All fifty shows sold out within five hours.

When Jackson returned to Los Angeles to begin rehearsals, AllGoodEntertainment Inc. reappeared, suggesting a one-off Jackson brothers reunion concert in 2010. Again, AEG and Jackson wanted nothing of this, and AllGood began proceedings to sue Jackson, stating that he was in breach of their original (if questionable) agreement.

Jackson announcing the concerts with UK TV personality Dermot O'Leary.

The preparations for *This Is It* began in earnest. This would rescue Jackson from artistic free fall, saving him from the feeling of being hemmed in by contracts and the very real realization that bankruptcy could be just around the corner. As Richards and Langthorne note in *83 Minutes*, "There wasn't much in Jackson's life at that point that was constant, except, perhaps, his financial turmoil."[5] This turmoil could be calmed, as long he was well enough to perform.

Nothing would be left to chance for the performances. Kenny Ortega, who had created and designed the *Dangerous* and *HIStory* world tours, was back to oversee everything. Rehearsals took place at Staples Center as well as at the Forum in Inglewood; the set list was going to run to between eighteen and twenty-two songs and come in at over two hours, with more than twenty set changes. As in his previous shows, Jackson would touch upon his whole

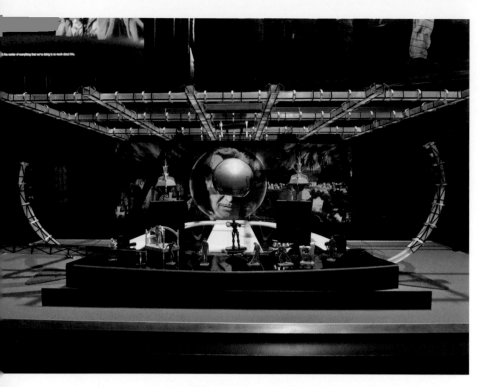

ABOVE: *The stage set, designed by Kenny Ortega, for* This Is It. BELOW: *Two of Jackson's sixteen costumes for the shows.* OPPOSITE: *"He certainly didn't exhibit any signs of being tired or not being with it." —Ken Ehrlich, 2009.*

career, and in the relentless twenty-first-century quest for "content," every rehearsal was filmed, providing vital footage for the concert film that was to appear after the tour had finished.

The best dancers and players were hired, such as Jonathan "Sugarfoot" Moffett on drums, Orianthi Panagaris on guitar, and Alex Al on bass, with keyboard player Michael Bearden as the music director. Fourteen dancers were brought in, and Ortega led an immediate production crew of fifteen. Jackson was to have sixteen different looks for the concerts. Zaldy, the New York fashion designer, was to be head costumier, creating ten of the looks, while Michael Bush and Dennis Tompkins created the others. Jackson's legendary white glove would be specially made for the concerts by Jay Ruckel.

Jackson, however, was alarmed at how many shows there were to be. Off the record, he had suggested that he felt the promoters were pushing him too hard. Director Ortega was concerned at Jackson's well-being and voiced his concerns to AEG, stating there were "strong signs of paranoia, anxiety, and obsessive-like behavior," before concluding, "I think the very best thing we can do is get a top psychiatrist to evaluate him ASAP."[6]

I USED TO GLANCE BEYOND THE STARS . . .

Shortly after midnight on June 25, 2009, Michael Jackson rehearsed "Earth Song" as the final song of the evening at the Staples Center. The night had been productive. The shows—now just fifteen days away—seemed to be coming to fruition, and the production was about to depart for London

> "This is the final curtain call, and I'll see you in July."
>
> —MICHAEL JACKSON

the following week. Worries about Jackson's health and stamina seemed to be allayed by the frequently electrifying performances he was putting in, even though he was working resolutely at half strength. Ken Ehrlich, an executive producer for the Grammys, had been present that evening to discuss the possibility of a future show with Jackson. He told CBS news, "He was really in good shape; he was very excited about the tour, very excited about getting it going. He certainly didn't exhibit any signs of being tired or not being with it."[7]

In the early hours of the morning, Jackson's car took him back to his rented mansion in the Holmby Hills. There, his personal physician, Conrad Murray, would be waiting for him to ensure that AEG's premier superstar would get a good night's sleep. Jackson went to bed at 1:30 a.m. Murray had been trying to wean Jackson off the anesthetic drug Propofol and instead administer more natural drugs and meditation to help the singer sleep. But Jackson knew that he wanted his "milk" to get him to sleep. His appearance at rehearsal the next day was central to the series of concerts continuing, which also meant it was central to Murray remaining in employment. At 10:40 a.m. on the morning of June 25, after a restless night, Murray began giving Jackson Propofol.

Michael Jackson's final stage performance: rehearsals for This Is It, *Staples Center, Los Angeles, June 2009.*

Jackson's frantic final months were all a reaction to the uncertain, frenzied period of country-hopping, partial recording, and litigation that had dogged him for the previous five years. Although his career had been in gradual commercial decline since the summit of Thriller, *the decision to make a prime-time TV documentary about his lifestyle was one of the most questionable in his entire career.* Living with Michael Jackson, *shown on ITV in the UK and ABC in the United States in February 2003, had a seismic effect on the already fragile Jackson.*

CHAPTER 2

DON'T WANT TO LIE DOWN IN A BED FULL OF LIES
LIVING WITH MICHAEL JACKSON

"Not everybody speak[s] English . . . [but] when you can have a melody, and everybody can hum a melody, then that's when it became France, the Middle East, everywhere! You have to be able to hum it, from the farmer in Ireland to the lady who scrubs toilets in Harlem to anybody who can whistle to a child poppin' their fingers."

—MICHAEL JACKSON, 2007[1]

The most troubled period of Michael Jackson's life emanated from his decision to be filmed by journalist Martin Bashir in a fly-on-the-wall documentary that looked at how he was living his life. Bashir had rapidly risen from the role of junior television newsman thanks to being part of the BBC *Newsnight* and *Panorama* teams. His *Panorama* interview with Princess Diana had been one of the most-watched in the world in 1995; his warm, unobtrusive style seemed to allow his subject to pour out her feelings. Jackson was drawn to Bashir because of this program; Diana was someone he deeply admired, and the pair had become friends after meeting in the mid-'80s.

The premise was simple: in the style of so many other early-2000s fly-on-the-wall documentaries, Bashir was to follow Jackson as he went about his business. Jackson is captured on film shopping, at the zoo, racing Bashir on the racetrack at Neverland; Bashir is probing in his line of questioning yet never forceful. In interview segments intercut with many of his classic tunes, Jackson opens up about songwriting and his life, and the two appear to be getting along well.

OPPOSITE: *Onstage at the World Music Awards, Earl's Court, London, November 2006.*

ABOVE AND RIGHT:
*Jackson shows
Bashir around his
studio.* OPPOSITE:
*Jackson shading
himself from Bashir's
line of questions.*

However, one key scene sees Jackson introduce the Arvizo children, who had been living at Neverland. One of the children, Gavin, is filmed with Jackson while talking about his recovery from cancer. Later, Gavin is shown with his head on Jackson's shoulder, and the two are holding hands. And then comes the bombshell, to an America already ready to find Jackson guilty: in the context of his relationship with Arvizo, Jackson tells Bashir that the "most loving thing you can do is to share your bed with someone." Jackson also talks about Gavin and his brother Star sleeping in his bed while he slept on the floor. (His children, Paris and Prince, and personal assistant Frank Tyson were in the room too.) He mentions other children sleeping in his bed as well.

Matters only become testy in the final sequence, when Bashir questions Jackson about his plastic surgery. Bashir then questions Jackson's sleeping arrangements. Jackson remonstrates, insisting that there was nothing untoward—*they were simply sleeping*.

Living with Michael Jackson was broadcast in early February 2003. The documentary attracted around fifteen million viewers in the UK and thirty million in the States. When Jackson saw it, he could not believe what he had just witnessed, and it sent him further into himself. His lawyers immediately sent complaints to the Broadcasting Standards Commission in the United States and the Independent Television Commission in the UK, insisting that the singer had been treated unfairly and his privacy infringed.

It seemed like another step on the path to his long-term destruction. "It broke him. It killed

him. He took a long time to die, but it started that night," then-manager Dieter Wiesner said. Jackson had had painkiller dependency issues in the wake of the burns he suffered from the Pepsi advert accident and then the legal proceedings against him in the '90s; they were about to worsen. "Previously, the drugs were a crutch," Wiesner continued, "but after that [*Living with Michael Jackson*] they became a necessity. I'll never forget the day at Neverland when he walked into the kitchen to eat. He was off his face; he couldn't even bring the fork up to his mouth. There he was, one of the most talented guys on the planet, unable to even eat because he was so doped up."[2]

The first thing that team Jackson did was mount a counteroffensive; the fun and games that Bashir and Jackson had enjoyed was all caught on tape, too, and another documentary could be made to show exactly how it really was. This documentary, *Michael Jackson: The Footage You Were Never Meant to See*, was shown on Fox on

February 20, arguing Jackson's case and painting the other side of the story. But the damage had been done; although the Arvizo family was initially loyal to Jackson, it has been said that after the documentary appeared he decided he would no longer support them financially. The family began legal proceedings against him. Arvizo's mother was allegedly unaware the film was being made, and Gavin complained that he was now being teased about it.

After hearing from Arvizo's family, Thomas W. Sneddon Jr., the District Attorney of Santa Barbara County—and the man who had presided over the Jordan Chandler case in 1993—obtained an indictment against Jackson.

NUMBER ONES

In the middle of all this, Jackson could still seek solace in what he loved the best. Returning to the recording studio, he cut a new track with R. Kelly, intended as an additional extra for a new greatest-hits project.

"One More Chance" is a beautiful slow number in the style of a classic ballad. It hit the Top 5 in the UK, and, emphasizing Jackson's global reach, topped the charts in Moldova, Turkey, and Venezuela. However, it only reached No. 83 in the United States—something that would once have been unthinkable for a brand new Michael Jackson single.

The video for the single was in the midst of being shot by director David Brandt when

Santa Barbara County Sheriff Jim Anderson (right) and District Attorney Thomas W. Sneddon Jr.

Jackson had to return to Los Angeles to deal with these new allegations of sexual misconduct. As a result, a montage video was released to accompany the song; the full video was not shown until 2010.

The accompanying hits album was inspired by similar collections by the Beatles and Elvis Presley, which distilled global phenomena into a single-CD collection of their biggest worldwide hits. This was clearly a club of which Jackson deserved to be a member. It should also be noted that the public still respected Jackson as a performer. *Number Ones* reached No. 1 in the UK and No. 13 in the United States, where compilation albums rarely chart highly.

As the *Number Ones* album was being released to customary fanfare around the world, Santa Barbara County Officers conducted a search of the Neverland Ranch. Speculation exploded across the media. As warrants for his arrest were being prepared, on November 20, Jackson flew in from Las Vegas and surrendered himself to the police. He was charged, under section 288(a) of California Penal Code, with "lewd or lascivious acts" with a child younger than fourteen. He posted $3 million bail.

CASE NO. 133603: THE PEOPLE OF THE STATE OF CALIFORNIA V. MICHAEL JOSEPH JACKSON

Michael Jackson was accused of sexual abuse against Gavin Arvizo: four counts of molesting a minor; one count of attempted child molestation; four counts of attempting to intoxicate a minor with a view to molest him; conspiring to commit child abduction and extortion; and, finally, looking to hold the boy and his family captive at Neverland.[3] It all made for grim reading.

The alleged period of molestation was between February 20 and March 12, which would have meant that it occurred after the Bashir documentary had aired. The trial began on January 31, 2005. Jackson and his family would turn up every day to the courthouse, as would the hardcore group of fans who cheered him on from outside.

As Caroline Sullivan noted in the *Guardian*,

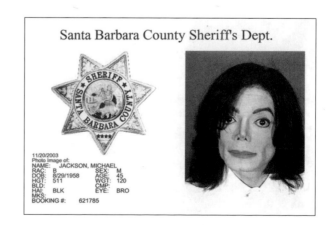

ABOVE: *Michael Jackson's fans stand strong and united outside the Santa Maria courthouse.* OPPOSITE: *Jackson stands on a car to thank his fans at his arraignment, Santa Maria, California, January 16, 2004.*

"During pre-trial hearings of his child-molestation case in 2004, fans outside the court waved banners reading 'Innocent Until Proved Innocent.' "[4] Bashir was called as a witness for the prosecution. As the trial progressed, Jackson's life was unpicked forensically. His private life and his financial affairs were minutely scrutinized. One morning he was made to come to the courthouse in his pajamas, as he had been hospitalized with a back complaint.

On June 13, 2005, Jackson was found not guilty of all ten felony and all four misdemeanor charges. On June 26, he issued a formal statement reflecting on the trail. "Without God, my children, my family, and you, my fans, I could not have made it through. Your love, support, and loyalty made it all possible. You were there when I really needed you, and I will never forget you. Your ever-present love held me, dried my tears, and carried me through. I will treasure your devotion and support forever. You are my inspiration."[5]

AFTERMATH AND RETREAT

As the trial came to its conclusion, it was as if Jackson simply disappeared into thin air. As the writer Joseph Vogel notes, "The one-time face of popular music has become a sort of vagabond, an artist in exile. Tabloids occasionally speculated on his whereabouts (Bahrain, Ireland, Las Vegas) or caught glimpses of him with his children in a bookstore or an amusement park. For the most part, though, he had slipped from the public's consciousness. Most assumed his career was over."[6] In April 2006, Sony refinanced Jackson's loans against the ATV catalogue in order to avert his financial collapse. For an artist, though, he simply wasn't producing any art.

As soon as the trial was over, Jermaine brokered an arrangement for Jackson and his family to live in Bahrain with his friend, Sheik Abdulla Hamad Al-Khalifa, a member of the Bahraini royal family, who had aspirations as a musician. Al-Khalifa gifted Jackson a $120,000 Rolls-Royce as a symbol of their friendship. It was announced that Jackson had signed an exclusive recording agreement with the sheik's Two Seas Records, and was working on new material, that was scheduled for release in late 2007. Furthermore, Jackson said, "I am incredibly excited about my new venture and I am enjoying being back in the studio making music."[7] It was said that the deal would comprise two albums, a potential musical, and an autobiography.

Guy Holmes, the UK head of independent label Gut Records, was announced as the label's CEO.

There is little denying that the period in Bahrain was good for Jackson, but soon, as was his wont, he simply disappeared, leaving a broken contract in his wake. When it became clear he wasn't returning, Al-Khalifa began considering legal proceedings.

EIRE, APPARENTLY

At the end of June, the Jackson family arrived in Cork, in western Ireland; they would live in the country on and off for the remainder of the year. Jackson had loved the reception he received when the *Bad* tour reached Cork in 1988, and he felt that this would be an ideal place to live anonymously. Soon, however, it became clear that Jackson could not be left alone anywhere.

There was talk that he would open a leprechaun-inspired theme park that he could twin with Neverland.

The family resided at four luxury hideaways: Blackwater Castle and Ballinacurra House in County Cork; the $30,000-a-week, 5,000-acre Luggala Castle in County Wicklow; and Grouse Lodge in County Westmeath. While Jackson was at Blackwater, owner Patrick Nordstrom tried to give the singer and his children "some normality from their crazy world. Having them in the house was a very normal experience in many ways, but it was also very weird. The children could play in the gardens because of the high walls. They really enjoyed it and you could tell they adored their father."[8]

Grouse Lodge had its own studio, and Jackson invited producers such as Rodney Jerkins to visit him; will.i.am of the Black Eyed Peas was

RIGHT: *"He Beat It!"—the newspapers report the verdict.* OPPOSITE: *Michael and Joe Jackson greet fans after the not-guilty verdict, June 2005.*

also asked by Jackson to work on tracks for a proposed follow-up to his 2001 album *Invincible*. An article published on *Today*'s Access Hollywood site showed a picture of a smiling Jackson sitting next to a pensive will.i.am at Grouse Lodge. Jackson looks clearly relieved to be back behind a mixing console after a troubled period in his life. Although he won the Arvizo case, it had damaged his standing, and there were a whole score of other princes in the waiting, ready to steal his crown.

For will.i.am, though, working with Michael was the ultimate accolade. Jackson had been the biggest figure in popular music for the best part of two decades, with a proven track record of working with the hottest producers and songwriters. At that point in time, in will.i.am, Jackson had both. He was reported as saying, "I think will's doing wonderful, innovative, positive, great music . . . I like what he is doing and thought it would be interesting to collaborate or just see how the chemistry worked."[9] The project was to continue, in a stop-start manner, for the next three years.

Will.i.am took every opportunity to discuss Jackson in the highest possible terms. In early 2009, he told www.hiphopdx.com, "Here it is: the nigga that did everything first. The first dude to have a video on MTV that really impacted pop culture. The first dude that ever said, 'When you do a video, this is how you dance in it.' The first dude to say, 'When you do a Pepsi commercial, this is how you do with brands.' . . . Michael Jackson . . . he really knows what the fuck he's talking about."[10]

Whatever missteps he took in his private life, Jackson was renowned for hooking up with the very best in the studio; among the songs that he and will.i.am were reportedly working on were "I'm Gonna Miss You" (dedicated to James Brown), "The Future," and "The King." As long-term follower Nelson George later wrote, "In that mass of music, you can bet there will be a gem or two that were left behind while Michael spent most of his focus on his precarious finances and gradually became a slave to debilitating medications."[11]

The Jackson family went to London in November, and on the 15th he gave what was to be his final public performance, singing a few lines of "We Are the World" at the World Music Awards at London's Earls Court Arena. That night, Jackson was presented with the Diamond Award by Beyoncé Knowles. The award recognized artists whose work had sold over one hundred million copies. In Jackson's case, *Thriller* alone had done that.

After a six-month stay in Ireland, Jackson returned to the United States, setting up home in Las Vegas, Nevada. Rumors began to circulate about a comeback, especially when he was spotted dining with choreographer and producer Kenny Ortega. There was also talk of him appearing on *American Idol* and linking up with Simon Cowell, but what Jackson was doing, simply, was working.

Rumors concerning Jackson's health and financial situation were exacerbated by his appearance on a subsequent visit to Europe: he looked ill, and it was reported that he was borrowing against his Sony/ATV catalogue to fund his lifestyle. It was reported in the media that he was either about to lose or sell his share in the publishing company. Details of a series of large and small unpaid bills seemed to suggest he was in a dire financial position. Jackson's publicist, Raymone Bain, seemed to be issuing a new statement every week to dispel one half-truth or another.

It was time to shine up the PR machine. Jackson's erratic behavior, such as making his children wear masks in public, can now be read as the actions of a man who had had lost every last shard of trust in the media that had made him. He had created his character; now he had to live with it. And he seemed to be having problems living with it.

FROM THE FARMER IN IRELAND TO THE LADY WHO SCRUBS TOILETS IN HARLEM: EBONY MAGAZINE

A great many people out there most definitely wanted the Michael Jackson of old back in their midst. In December 2007, Epic Records, through its heritage wing, Legacy, announced a special twenty-fifth-anniversary edition of *Thriller* for release in 2008, following on from the success of the "Special Editions" of *Off the Wall* and *Thriller* in 2001. The

At the World Music Awards with Beyoncé in 2006. She said on his passing: "The reason I am here is due to Michael Jackson."

next year would thankfully begin with a return to the music—and the music that everyone loved.

To coincide with the announcement of *Thriller 25*, Michael Jackson gave a one-off interview to *Ebony* magazine. Conducted by the magazine's editorial director, the award-winning journalist Bryan Monroe, it was the first interview he had given since his 2005 trial and acquittal. Jackson seemed relaxed and eager to stress quite how busy he had been.

"I'm writing a lot of stuff right now," he told Monroe. "I'm in the studio, like, every day." Some contemporary music, he felt, like rap, would have a limited global appeal because "not everybody speak[s] English . . . [but] when you can have a melody, and everybody can hum a melody, then that's when it became France, the Middle East, everywhere! You have to be able to hum it, from the farmer in Ireland to the lady who scrubs toilets in Harlem to anybody who can whistle to a child poppin' their fingers."[12] Jackson's pop sensibility would never leave him. He seemed happy to talk about his success and go right back to the early days.

The article, published in the December 2007, was the final print interview Michael Jackson would ever give.

Martin Bashir's Living with Michael Jackson *documentary only amplified the turmoil in which Michael Jackson found himself. Money worries, issues with his management, and his relationships were all on his mind. He was often at his happiest creating in the studio, and, back in 2001, he knew he needed to make an album that would put him back at the forefront of popular music. Working again to high production, songwriting, and sonic standards, he achieved the unthinkable with* Invincible—a *Michael Jackson album that, although it sold in its millions, was released to a wave of indifference.*

CHAPTER 3

STAY WITH ME, FULFILL MY DREAMS

INVINCIBLE

"The songwriting process is something very difficult to explain because it's very spiritual. . . . I feel guilty having to put my name, sometimes, on the songs. I do write them. I compose them, I write them, I do the scoring, I do the lyrics, I do the melodies but still . . . it's a work of God."

—MICHAEL JACKSON[1]

The final year of the century that he had helped shape culturally was a relatively low-key one for Michael Jackson: a mixture of widescreen gestures, awards ceremonies, and crushing mundaneness. It was as if he became a nomadic presence around the globe, picking up awards and appearing In places that were so incongruous that one would almost have to pinch oneself to believe they were actually witnessing *the* Michael Jackson.

In April 1999, Jackson went to watch an English soccer game at Fulham FC in London with his friend, the controversial former owner of Harrods, Mohamed Al Fayed. He was in town as Al Fayed's guest, and spoke to fans for over an hour outside his apartment in London. In contrast, in May, Jackson received a Bollywood Award from the Indian Film Industry for "World Humanity"; in August, he was given the New Millennium Visionary Award, presented by Whitney Houston on behalf of the American Cinema Awards Foundation.

In June, Jackson staged three "Michael Jackson and Friends" concerts in Seoul, South Korea, and Munich, Germany, in order to raise money for impoverished children around the world. Jackson himself played a short set; guests across the nights included Andrea Bocelli, Luther Vandross, Vanessa Mae, erstwhile Guns N' Roses guitarist

OPPOSITE: *Michael Jackson in the unlikely setting of Craven Cottage, Fulham FC's ground in London, with Mohamed Al Fayed.*

Slash, André Rieu, Status Quo, Ringo Starr, All Saints, and Boyz II Men.

During his performance at the Olympic Stadium in Munich, on June 27, the central section of the "bridge of no return," from which he sang "Earth Song" high above the stage, collapsed, sending him crashing to the floor at enormous speed. Ever the professional, he didn't even skip a beat; he kept on singing. After the song, he went offstage and collapsed in his dressing room, before being taken to the hospital. Since spending time in rehab back in 1993, Jackson had returned

to taking Demerol to ease his pain, but after this incident, he was administered Propofol under the direction of his physician, Dr. Allan Metzger.

In September, he received a Lifetime Achievement Award from Nelson Mandela at the Kora All African Music Awards in Sun City, where he handed over a check for one million rand (around $300,000 at the time) to the Mandela Children's Fund: the proceeds from the Michael Jackson and Friends concerts.

On October 8, 1999, Jackson and Debbie Rowe, his wife of three years, divorced. It had been, to say the least, an unusual relationship. They had been great friends, and she bore his children, but they had lived apart, and it was clear that Jackson was still deeply in love with his first wife, Lisa Marie Presley. Rowe received a settlement in the region of $10 million and a house in Beverly Hills.

As the twentieth century ended and the twenty-first got underway, Jackson topped a series of low-key compilations and polls, emphasizing his continuing importance. On March 2, 2001, he was inducted into the Rock and Roll Hall of Fame; at forty-two, he was the youngest

OPPOSITE: *Jackson receives a Lifetime Achievement Award from Nelson Mandela, Sun City, South Africa, September 1999.* BELOW: *Jackson's induction into the Rock And Roll Hall of Fame, March 2001.*

solo artist ever to receive that honor. He appeared with walking sticks, as he had damaged his foot while rehearsing, fueling more press speculation about his well-being. The world-circling continued as he appeared at functions in Germany and the UK. He gave a speech to Oxford University's Union on March 6, which he used to launch his Heal the Kids charity. However, the majority of time was taken up by work on his new album, his tenth. More than ever, he had something to prove.

INVINCIBLE?

To herald the release of this new album, two special fund-raising concerts were announced for September 7 and 10, 2001, at New York's Madison Square Garden. They were put together by David Gest, Jackson's friend and the soon-to-be husband of Liza Minnelli, and aired in November on CBS as *Michael Jackson: 30th Anniversary Celebration.*

Billed as Jackson's "first US mainland performances in eleven years"—clearly his 1993 Super Bowl performance did not count—the shows reportedly had the most expensive ticket prices of all time at the time: the best seats were sold at $10,000, and Jackson was rumored to have bagged $7.5 million for each show. It was a glittering pair of nights in front of a star-studded crowd. Artists ranging from Luther Vandross to Kenny Rogers sang his songs, while Jackson performed duets with artists such as Britney Spears, Slash, and Usher, and then did what he had vowed never to do: he reunited with his brothers onstage.

The concerts were a remarkable success and showed that the appetite for Jackson was still there. After the second concert, however,

ABOVE: *Jackson with Britney Spears at one of two of his 30th Anniversary Special concerts, Madison Square Garden, New York City, 2001.*
RIGHT: *The Jacksons reunite at the 30th Anniversary Special concerts.*

thousands of fans were left stranded in the city the next morning. The global mindset would change forever following the terror attacks on the World Trade Center and the Pentagon, which resulted in nearly three thousand deaths. On September 16, Jackson announced a charity single, "What More Can I Give," with proceeds going to a relief fund for the survivors and victims' families.

Like many other artists at the time—especially those, like him, who had a longstanding professional relationship with the city—Jackson felt an overriding need to "do something," and on October 21, at the RFK Stadium in Washington, DC, he put together the *United We Stand—What More Can I Give* show in front of 54,000 people. Performers included Rod Stewart, James Brown, Carole King, Pink, Jan Hammer, and *NSYNC; Jackson closed the show with "We Are the World" and "Man in the Mirror," before the amassed artists all returned to sing "What More Can I Give."

It could be said that 9/11 overshadowed the

Jackson at the United We Stand—What More Can I Give *concert on October 21, 2001.*

release of *Invincible*, Jackson's first album of entirely new material since 1991's *Dangerous* (one LP of the double-disc *HIStory* was a greatest-hits set). It certainly clouded the release of the lead single, "You Rock My World." The thirteen-minute video for the song premiered on September 21; had it been a stronger song, and a different time, Jackson could just about have begun to dance America—and the world—out of

its deep, sorrowful shock. As it was, "You Rock My World" was a cool, swaggering slice of R&B, co-produced with Rodney "Darkchild" Jerkins, that was not released as a commercial single in the United States, and therefore made only No. 10 on the *Billboard* Hot 100—not what one would once have expected from the first new Michael Jackson single in four years.

Invincible was a tremendously workmanlike entrée into the twenty-first century. The whole album proceeds forward on its platinum wheels, and is perfectly well-designed, yet the world was turning; the pop market was in thrall to groups such as *NSYNC and Destiny's Child, with their new pop-savvy soulfulness. Was there still room for Jackson?

Invincible was rumored at the time to be the most expensive album ever made, with well over one hundred people contributing to its inception, at an alleged cost of some $30 million. As if leaving nothing to chance, Jackson was joined in the production chair by a "who's who" of millennial R&B and hip-hop pioneers: Teddy Riley returned, and was joined by Dr. Freeze, Andre Harris, Babyface, R. Kelly, Andreao "Fanatic" Heard, Nate Smith, and Richard Stites, along, of course, with Rodney "Darkchild" Jerkins.

Invincible was a cool, calculated album; released on October 29, it came in a selection of five different color covers, all showcasing a close head shot in gold, green, red, silver, or blue. It is a record with many outstanding moments. Opener "Unbreakable" features a beyond-the-grave rap from the Notorious B.I.G.; "Heartbreaker" is another groove, co-written with Rodney Jerkins; "Speechless," inspired by the fun that Jackson had enjoyed having during a water-balloon fight with children in Germany, is a touching moment, and, on an album where most songs have an average running time of just under five minutes, is blessedly brief at just over three.

The album is a snapshot of Jackson's life at the time; the embittered rant at the media, "Privacy," is offset by "You Are My Life," a tender ballad for his children. The album contains echoes of the past throughout: closing track "Threatened" featured a recorded speech by Rod Serling, the man behind the US TV chiller *The Outer Limits*, making it a satisfying distant relative of "Thriller."

One of the truly outstanding songs of Jackson's career can be found on the album. "Whatever Happens" was buried as the fifteenth track out of sixteen. Written by Jasmine Quay, Geoffrey Williams, and Gil Cang, it arrives as a soulful plea, showcasing Jackson's outstanding sensitivity as a vocalist, and is made all the more remarkable by the presence of Carlos Santana on guitar. Santana and Jackson had both broken through in the same year, 1969. As a result, it is a memorable record that truly hits the right spots. "I was very honored that he called on me to work with him, and I love the song," Santana told MTV.[2]

The reviews for *Invincible* were mixed; many suggested that it suffered from the great millennial issue of there being simply *too much music*, the result of a desire to fill up all eighty minutes of a CD's running time. The *New York Times* called it "a general return—post-grunge, post-gangsta—to peppy, happy-faced pop songs: a reaction to too much self-important gloomy music."[3] The ever-iconoclastic *NME* from Great Britain said, "At 76 minutes and 16 tracks, the studio clearly never rang with the dreaded words 'no, Michael.' There's about five too many bollocks R. Kellyish soul ballads featuring 'drumming' that resembles someone slapping a wet

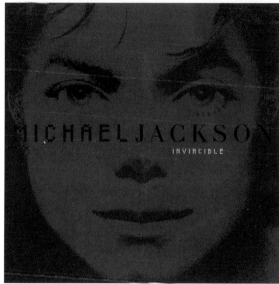

ferret with a stick and the record predictably slides into blubbing-billionaire sentimentality halfway through."[4] Harsh, but not totally untrue.

Invincible sold three million copies worldwide within five days; in several European countries, it broke records, becoming Jackson's fastest-selling album ever. In the United States alone, the album sold 366,300 copies in its first week and entered the charts straight at the top spot. But, unlike its predecessors, what the album didn't have was an afterlife. It became a classic example of a fan-club record, selling to the hardcore but not then radiating out to the wider public and being sustained by ongoing hit singles. The great news for Jackson was that his fan club was enormous; he was hardly a cult artist. It was later argued that, after selling thirteen million copies worldwide, Sony stopped promoting *Invincible*, barely marketing the follow-up singles "Butterflies" and "Cry." *Invincible* would go on to be seen as a relative commercial disappointment when compared to Jackson's prior solo material. Jackson refused to tour it, and was in dispute with label boss Tommy Mottola. Within a year, Sony—which had been in dispute with Jackson about the ownership of his master tapes— declined to renew his recording contract.

A NEW CHILD AND A VISIT TO THE WEST COUNTRY

Michael Jackson became a father for the third time when Prince Michael "Blanket" Jackson II was born in La Mesa, California, on February 21, 2002. The identity of Blanket's mother, a surrogate, has yet to be revealed.

On June 14, 2002, with *Invincible* having long since begun sliding down the world's charts,

Michael Jackson appeared at the English soccer club Exeter's stadium with his friend, the mystic spoon-bender Uri Geller, also the co-chairman of the club at the time. (Geller had also provided illustrations for both *Blood on the Dance Floor* and *Invincible*.) As the *Guardian* newspaper reported, the trip, which was unusual to say the least, was "boasted some stellar names: the hungry, box-dwelling, pole-balancer David Blaine; the soul diva Patti Boulaye; and, at the top of the bill, the world-famous Michael Jackson, the King of Pop."[5]

Jackson agreed to help raise funds for the ailing club on the grounds that at least half of the proceeds went to AIDS research. He stood on a makeshift stage at the city's St. James Park and told the amassed crowd to hold hands: "I mean it! Right now! Go ahead! Don't be shy. Do it! Do it! Now, tell the person next to you that you care for them. Tell them that you love them. This is what makes the difference! Together we can make a change to the world. Together we can help to stop racism. Together we can help to stop prejudice. We can help the world live without fear." The bemused crowd did as they were told.

Jackson had clearly got the bug, and was subsequently named as an honorary director of the football club. The BBC reported with glee, "Jackson is now entitled to play a full part in the club's boardroom, including voting on key decisions about players. He will also enjoy free admission to any games he may want to attend, and will be able to travel to away matches with the players on the club coach."[6]

Meanwhile, Blanket, the young brother of Prince and Paris, leaped into the world's consciousness on November 19, when his father briefly dangled him over the fourth-floor balcony

A curious lineup: David Blaine, Michael Jackson, and Uri Geller at an Exeter City FC match, June 2002.

of the Presidential Suite of the Hotel Adlon in Berlin in front of a small crowd of fans. Jackson's eccentricity appeared to be escalating. Although he seemed to be playing the role of being peculiar to the masses, this was arguably a step too far. He quickly issued a statement. "I offer no excuses for what happened. I made a terrible mistake. I got caught up in the excitement of the moment. I would never intentionally endanger the lives of my children."[7]

Michael Jackson and children: he loved them so much, yet, being so childlike himself, he could make what other adults would deem glaring errors of judgment regarding his relationship with them. It was all about to get out of hand.

If Invincible *heralded the finale of Michael Jackson as a world-conquering, groundbreaking artist, the period before was a time of defiant hubris, with Jackson doing all he could to defy his detractors with his* HIStory *releases. His personal life, too, was under intense scrutiny and debate, all of which fed into his work. This seemed to be a nonstop period of divorce, marriage, childbirth, touring, filmmaking, recording, and writing.*

CHAPTER 4

I AM HERE WITH YOU

HISTORY

"I don't think he's facing an image problem; I think the music will make the statement."

—DAVID GLEW, FORMER CHAIRMAN OF EPIC RECORDS[1]

"He's probably the most famous person on the planet, God help him."

—BOB GELDOF, INTRODUCING JACKSON AT THE 1996 BRIT AWARDS[2]

Like a slow-moving vehicle reversing out of a narrow street, the Jackson juggernaut continued dispensing its message across the world—and, in the main, the world lapped it up. The hubris of sailing a thirty-foot statue of his likeness right up the River Thames in London, requiring Tower Bridge to open, marked the moment throughout the world, even if people were not aware already, that Jackson truly became the King of Pop. Although various coronations had happened across the years, only two had really stuck: Elvis Presley as the "King of Rock 'n' Roll" and Aretha Franklin as the "Queen of Soul." Jackson had been bestowed the title in 1989 by Elizabeth Taylor; this seemed to be his formal coronation. It was an aggressive assertion of his superiority.

Jackson's first release since the Jordan Chandler scandal had to be big and bold. Released on June 16, 1995, *HIStory: Past, Present, and Future, Book 1*—to give the double album its full title—was all of these things. And, if a reminder was needed, the first disc of *HIStory* was a greatest-hits set, underlining his superiority and track record. That old material was subtitled *HIStory Begins*, while the fifteen tracks of new material on the second disc was entitled *HIStory Continues*.

It could be argued that the new material was not enough on its own to sell in the quantities that Sony—or indeed Jackson—would require, but that was far from the case. Epic, under new Chairman David Glew, had asked Jackson if it could release a greatest-hits album in time for Christmas 1994; Jackson had already begun working on new

OPPOSITE: *Jackson rehearsing for the MTV Video Music Awards, September 1995.*

"An aggressive assertion of his superiority." Jackson's statue sails through Tower Bridge, London, June 1995.

songs and told Glew to hold off, as he wanted to complete the new songs first. The hits disc, sequenced for feel rather than chronology, offers a glimpse into arguably *the* greatest performer of his generation, as if to serve as a reminder of what he had produced and what shouldn't be lost.

The new material on the *HIStory Continues* disc was written by Jackson in collaboration with a phalanx of writers and producers, and was recorded in a relatively short burst from September 1994 to March 1995. It also ramped up all of the themes of Jackson's recent work: mainly paranoia but also isolation and, very pointedly, injustice. Although Quincy Jones was long gone, engineer Bruce Swedien was still present to take care of his charge, working with Bill Bottrell, among other producers.

"I noticed a difference as the albums we worked together on progressed but his musicality never wavered," Swedien told me in 2009. "With Michael, the musical boundaries were always very wide, no matter how you looked at it." The studio increasingly became a place for Jackson to escape, to retreat back to what he knew. "I set up a room for him in the studio, where he had all his stuff in there and he could go in there and keep everybody out. He used to take a nap every day for forty-five minutes and he'd lock the damn door! I used to worry that there would be a fire, but he told me repeatedly not to worry. He was a little out there."[3]

So, the new material the world was waiting for: could Jackson still do it? Would it be full of clues and swipes at his detractors? The answer to these questions seemed to be a resounding "yes." In fact,

Hot 100 began. That was where it peaked, however; it was an amazing statement record, but unlike Jackson's best-known work, it rather lacked in the kind of melody that would take it beyond the most fervent Jackson supporters.

It was to be a very different picture with the second release from the album, "You Are Not Alone," which became the first single in *Billboard* history to debut at No. 1, and was the thirteenth and final US No. 1 of Jackson's lifetime. The song was written for him by R. Kelly, and together the two created a ballad that has become an outstanding fan favorite.

Elsewhere on the album, "They Don't Care About Us" sees guitarist Trevor Rabin taking the Eddie Van Halen/Steve Stevens role. The ex-Yes man contributes to a song that was to prove most controversial for Jackson, since supposedly it contained an anti-Semitic rant. What this showed was that whatever he did, Jackson seemed increasingly to be imprisoned in a world of his own making. In suggesting that he

all of those issues were answered on the album's lead single, "Scream," a duet with sister Janet, with the repeated refrain "stop pressurin' me." "Scream" was recorded with producers Jimmy Jam and Terry Lewis, who had worked extensively with Janet and been largely responsible for bringing a soulful warmth to the mechanization of beats with their work from 1986 onward. Written by Jackson, his sister, and Jam and Lewis, "Scream" was a direct reaction against the allegations that had been leveled at him since he last made a record. Its release was also accompanied by one of the most expensive promo clips ever made. Directed by Mark Romanek, who had recently worked with David Bowie, Madonna, and R.E.M., it is set on a spaceship; filmed in black-and-white, it displays a hitherto unseen playfulness between the siblings and toys with image and gender issues. And lots of zero gravity.

When "Scream" was released as a single in May 1995, it set US chart records as it entered at No. 5, making it the highest new entry since the *Billboard*

ABOVE: The "Scream" single launched the HIStory project in May 2005. BELOW: Yes, that really is Elvis Presley's daughter in the nude with Michael Jackson: the "You Are Not Alone" video.

ABOVE: "Earth Song" was to become Jackson's unassailable theme for the last decade and a half of his life; this is a still from the video for the song. OPPOSITE: Jackson's simple black suit, as first modeled on Off The Wall, was never far from his concert wardrobe.

the injustices to young people and how the system can wrongfully accuse them. I am angry and outraged that I could be so misinterpreted."[4] Jackson re-recorded the words as "do me" and "strike me"; there was clear talk of double standards in the music industry.

"D.S."—with Slash on guitar—is a surprisingly vicious, thinly veiled attack on Santa Barbara District Attorney Thomas Sneddon. Jackson had escaped his grasp, but Sneddon's influence would continue to inform his work for the next decade. (The repeated chorus of "Dom Sheldon is a cold man" is sung in such an onomatopoeic way that it could sound like he is saying "Tom Sneddon.")

The lushly orchestrated—complete with children's choir—"Childhood," heard already on the Free Willy 2 soundtrack, is a tearful, Disney-esque paean to that which Jackson so craved ("no one understands me"), with the pointed lyric "before you judge me, try hard to love me." "Money" and "Tabloid Junkie" are effectively rants. Boosting his own income, Jackson finally recorded a version of the Beatles' "Come Together," Lennon and McCartney's Abbey Road classic for which he had co-owned the publishing rights since his purchase of ATV in 1985, and which he had been playing live for years.

The intricate and extensive "Earth Song" would become the song most closely identified with Jackson in his later career. It is an enormous proclamation about the state of the planet—the sort of record that would endear him to his followers and fuel his detractors. In many ways, it is the logical conclusion of the work started with "We Are the World." It was originally intended for the Dangerous album but was left off because

was the victimized underdog, his crude parallel with Judaism (in particular the lines "Jew me" and "Kike me") raised concerns and immediately caused a furor in the press. Jackson was quick to clarify that "the idea that these lyrics could be deemed objectionable is extremely hurtful to me, and misleading. The song, in fact, is about the pain of prejudice and hate, and is a way to draw attention to social and political problems. I am the voice of the accused and the attacked. I am the voice of everyone. I am the skinhead, I am the Jew, I am the black man, I am the white man. I am not the one who was attacking. It is about of its similarity to "Heal the World." British bass player Guy Pratt played on the sessions and later recalled Jackson hiding under the mixing desk through shyness, calling up from underneath to tell producer Bill Bottrell what Pratt should do. It was undoubtedly an absolutely enormous song, clearly destined for anthem status.

The album closes with "Smile," one of those unmistakable Michael Jackson moments of up-close sincerity. Taking the Charlie Chaplin standard and making it his own, it was one of his very favorite performances.

The worldwide marketing campaign for the album was based around a statue of Jackson, in his full military regalia, standing proud, looking into the distance. Created by Diana Walczak, it was used on the album's sleeve, and then a mold of it was made to create the thirty-foot statues, weighing in at 20,000 pounds, that were used to market the album and the tour. Aside from the one that was towed up the River Thames in London, another stood atop the Tower Records Shop in Los Angeles; one was lowered by a crane into place in the Alexanderplatz in Berlin; another appeared on the Champs-Elysées in Paris. Jackson was mounting an enormous peacetime invasion of his territories.

DIVORCE FROM PRESLEY

It was a heightened time. As *HIStory* was released, Jackson's relationship with Lisa Marie Presley was under intense scrutiny. During the recording of the album, they had lived in a duplex in Trump Tower in New York; otherwise, they visited each other's homes. But as time passed, it became apparent that, aside from their intense

sexual relationship, they were at each other's throats. Jackson also desperately wanted children of his own. His stepchildren by Lisa Marie were distant to him, but she was rightly concerned about bringing a child into an unstable union.

The marriage was causing Jackson an acute level of stress. In December 1995, during rehearsals for a televised show at the Beacon Theater New York, Jackson collapsed and had to be hospitalized. Presley initially refused to fly from L.A. to be by his side. When she did eventually arrive, she

ABOVE: *Jackson with Guns N' Roses guitarist, Slash, at the 1995 MTV Video Music Awards.* OPPOSITE: *Jackson shooting the video for "They Don't Care About Us" in Rio, 1996.*

could barely contain her contempt for him. They argued while he lay in his hospital bed, to the point where she was forbidden to be in the room on the grounds of his health. It effectively ended the marriage. On January 18, 1996, less than two years since their wedding, the marriage between Michael and Lisa Marie Presley was over. Their divorce was made official on August 20.

"EARTH SONG" AT THE BRITS

While Jackson was recovering from his mystery illness, and separated from his wife, "Earth Song" became an effortless UK No. 1 for Christmas 1995. Ironically, it kept one of the few Beatles songs for which he didn't own the publishing off pole position: the maudlin John-Lennon-beyond-the-grave reunion "Free as a Bird."

And "Earth Song" continued selling, having an enormous resonance with UK audiences in a way it didn't in the United States, where it was only released as a radio track, as opposed to a physical single. By 2013, it had sold 1.17 million units, becoming Jackson's only million-selling single in the UK. It also topped the charts in Switzerland, Italy, Sweden, and Spain, and was his first No. 1 single in Germany, too.

The messianic promo video, directed by Nick Brandt, graphically depicts the song's strong environmental theme, climaxing with Jackson bringing together the world's people and reversing the impact of war and global warming. The video was shot in the Amazon rainforest, to show effects of deforestation; a war zone in Croatia; Tanzania, to highlight poaching; and New York State, to demonstrate a forest fire. By its very scale and largesse, it was the sort of video that was made to win awards—and win it did.

The Jackson wagon rolled into the UK in February 1996, when he was booked to appear at the sixteenth BRIT Awards and be crowned "Artist of a Generation." Amid a show that featured live performances by Alanis Morissette, David Bowie and the Pet Shop Boys, Simply Red, and Take That, Jackson performed "Earth Song." Bob Geldof, who had worked with Jackson on "Heal the World," presented the award to him, saying, "They had to dream up an award to give him tonight, so they came up with the 'Artist of a Generation' award . . . when Michael Jackson sings, it is with the voice of angels, and when his feet move, you can see God dancing."

After Jackson thanked his fans, he returned to perform "Earth Song" in a live reenactment of the video onstage at London's Earl's Court arena.

As it progressed further, Jackson was raised on a platform and struck a Christlike pose. But while the performance would work well with global audiences, it did not sit well with the British sense of cynicism, humility, and understatement. It was certainly at odds with Jarvis Cocker, the front man from the UK group Pulp. Seated at the front of the stage, he could take no more, and, egged on by Pulp's keyboard player, Candida Doyle, he ran onto the stage with his friend Peter Mansell.

Cocker bent over, showed his behind, and pretended to break wind and waft the smell over the audience. One of Jackson's dancers confronted him, and then he was bundled offstage. In the ensuing fracas, it was rumored that Cocker had hit some children. Cocker was later to say, "My actions

were a form of protest at the way Michael Jackson sees himself as some kind of Christlike figure with the power of healing. The music industry allows him to indulge his fantasies because of his wealth and power. People go along with it even though they know it's a bit sick. I just couldn't go along with it anymore. It was a spur-of-the-moment decision brought on by boredom and frustration."[5]

Later, at a press conference, Cocker added, "He can dance . . . anybody who invents the moonwalk is alright by me . . . my feelings toward him now is that it would be good for him to get a bit of reality into his life."[6] Jackson replied that he was "sickened, saddened, shocked, upset, cheated, and angry." It was a strange episode that lost Jackson some of his common appeal in the UK, with many people believing that Cocker had been right.

LEFT: *"Earth Song" being performed at the Brit Awards, 1996. While Jackson's Christlike pose would go down well with global audiences . . .* ABOVE: *. . . it didn't with Pulp singer Jarvis Cocker, who jumped on stage and pretended to break wind.*

MARRIAGE TO DEBBIE ROWE

On November 14, 1996, less than three months after divorcing Lisa Marie Presley, Michael Jackson married Debbie Rowe. She had been his dermatology nurse (Presley had dismissively dubbed her "Nursey"), and Jackson had developed a crush on her. She was a fan who would fuss over him. She had been there to attend to his scrotum in the mid-'80s after he had burned it using the Benoquin bleaching cream that had been recommended to counter his vitiligo and acne. Although she was not his type, Rowe was a great friend who wanted to help Jackson, and she wanted to help in any way she could. She told him, "You deserve to be a father. Let me do this for you. Let me have your baby."[7]

In 1996, it was announced that Rowe was pregnant—widely rumored to be through artificial insemination. Shortly thereafter, she and Jackson were married, mainly to placate his mother, Katherine. Three months after the union, Michael Joseph Jackson Jr. was born, on February 13, 1997. He was to be known as Prince.

"I have been blessed beyond comprehension," Jackson announced, "and I will work tirelessly at being the best father I can be."[8] Debbie Rowe was effectively an affectionate surrogate mother.

THE HISTORY TOUR AND BLOOD ON THE DANCE FLOOR

While all this was happening, Jackson was back to the simple business of doing what he did best: entertaining stadiums full of fans with the magic of his music. The first leg of the *HIStory* tour began in September 1996, in Prague. It was a huge undertaking. Jackson's final tour was full of what people would expect from him onstage: a huge concert, packed with hits and stunning visual effects. Because of his treatment by the media as a result of the Chandler case, the tour did not visit North America. The eighty-five-date tour grossed $4.5 million and played, over two legs, fifty-nine cities in thirty-six countries.

When the tour reached the UK, in July 1997, Jackson played the Don Valley Stadium in Sheffield. Reviewing the show for Uncut, Paul Lester wrote, "Michael Jackson is under siege. A recent *National Enquirer* story indicated his increasing despair at the malice of his detractors. This is the most critical juncture of a career that has outstripped the achievements of the all-time greats. His one 'mistake'? Not dying."[9]

As the tour progressed, the new material that Jackson had been recording surfaced on the curious hybrid album *Blood on the Dance Floor:*

HIStory in the Mix. Released on May 20, 1997, the album contained five new songs and eight remixes from *HIStory*. For the first time since the days of high-period contract-filling Motown churn, this Michael Jackson album felt like something of a short-change exercise.

As Jackson biographer Chris Roberts wrote at the time, "The King of Pop doesn't make albums any more: he makes marketing concepts. Thus *HIStory*, which was rather good, was joined at the hip to a greatest hits collection, which was sensational. Each would have made more impact alone. The danger of such Zen sales projections, which have their head up their own niche, is that a 'new' Michael Jackson record, in being only 'half-new,' becomes less of a media event."[10]

This time, instead of a new album sitting alongside a greatest hits, here we had what seemed like some offcuts rubbing shoulders with some effective if not startling mixes by artists such as David Morales, Wyclef Jean, and Jam and Lewis (whose "Scream Louder" effectively mixes Sly Stone's "Thank You (Fallettinme Be Mice Elf Agin" with "Scream"). Roberts continued, "The

breaths, the whoops, the groin-clutches are back and proud. There are moments hereabouts where you realize it's amazing how unseriously we take this possessed, pulsatile nu-soul singer."[11]

Blood on the Dance Floor: HIStory in the Mix faired indifferently in the United States. It was under-promoted; already, Sony had begun to realize that Jackson's reach was truly global, and thus decided to concentrate less on the home market. The title track was a robust funk that topped the charts in the UK and helped the album become one the biggest-selling remix albums of all time. Even on half-strength, Jackson was able to generate another first. Of the remainder of the new material, "Morphine" has to be one of the strangest songs that Jackson ever committed to tape; over its industrial vigor, it breaks down to weave the tale of Demerol dependency; clearly, we have moved some way from "Wanna Be

OPPOSITE: *"You deserve to be a father. Let me do this for you." —Debbie Rowe, 1996.* **TOP:** *HIStory combined a new album with a post-Jacksons greatest hits album; it effortlessly reasserted Jackson's authority.* **ABOVE:** *Blood on the Dance Floor: HIStory in the Mix, an unusual hybrid of new material and remixes.*

Startin' Something." Three minutes in, the noise stops and the song becomes a ballad paean to the opioid pain medication. This is bizarre—almost as bizarre as the film that Jackson made that acted as a long-form video for the album.

"YOU'RE WEIRD, YOU'RE STRANGE —AND I DON'T LIKE YOU."

Michael Jackson's Ghosts, entered into the *Guinness Book of World Records* as the world's longest music video, is a heavy-handed take on a witch-hunt—a dramatization of the events that had surrounded Jackson since the Jordan Chandler case. Another stab at the horror genre, it was directed by Stan Winston and written with Stephen King.

The film starts with a rabble descending *en masse* to "Normal Valley" and a lonely mansion entitled "Someplace Else." The rabble is led by the mayor (played by Jackson under prosthetics), noted for his similarity to Thomas Sneddon, the District Attorney of Santa Barbara. The kids at the gate say to the Sneddon figure, "Why can't we just leave him alone, he hasn't hurt anybody, cant we just go?" Another child turns and says, "It's your fault, jerk, you just couldn't keep your mouth shut." The child's mother interjects, adding, "He did the right thing," before the attorney says, "He's a weirdo; there's no place in this town for weirdos."

As the lynch mob is drawn into the mansion, all the doors are bolted behind them; as they are led to a room, we see where the Maestro (Jackson) resides. He appears in a death mask before revealing his face with a telling question: "Did I scare you?" The Maestro is to be railroaded out of town by the attorney, because "we don't need

freaks like you telling 'em ghost stories . . . scaring these kids . . . back to the circus, you freak."

The Maestro declares that it is "game time": the first person from the gathering to be scared has to leave. All the kids respond to him, yet the adults fail to comprehend. A scare-off ensues, ending with Jackson removing his face, leaving just a skull, which he smashes and returns to his face. His army of ghosts joins him, and then the videos begin: "2 Bad" (from *HIStory*) and "Is It Scary" (from the recent album). Jackson strips down to reveal his skeleton—the ultimate act of transparency. How can a skeleton have anything to hide? Anyone viewing the film with even a modest grasp of current affairs could be in little doubt that this was a reference to the strip search he endured four years previously, still raw in his mind.

Jackson's spirit enters the mayor via his throat. And then Jackson, as the mayor, starts to lead the dance to the main song of the video, "Ghosts." The mayor himself turns into the biggest freak of all. The Maestro then leaves the mayor's body, before asking the children directly if they wish him to remain in the town. As the mayor spits "yes, yes," all the little children shake their heads, suggesting the opposite.

The Maestro, we discover, was made of stone and begins crumbling away, before returning through the door to finally finish off the mayor as he shatters through the windows. Everybody was scared, but they had a good time. However, a death-masked figure returns behind Jackson: the kid who reported him in the first place, on the shoulders of his friend, asking, "Did I scare you?" The final payoff is the kid's brother pulling his mouth wide open, in an update on the final twist of the *Michael Jackson's Thriller* video.

The film was released in a thirty-nine-minute cut (almost exactly three times the length of *Thriller*). It rattles along nicely, and, a decade previously, a product of such quality and notoriety would have been world headline news. Now, it merely seemed quaint. The world had caught up with Jackson's innovation. *Michael Jackson's Ghosts* was shown at the 1997 Cannes Film Festival and then opened in the United States in October 1997; it was also shown at the Odeon Leicester Square in London to tie in with the release of *Blood on the Dance Floor: HIStory in the Mix.*

WE'LL ALWAYS HAVE PARIS

Some nine months after Jackson and Rowe visited Disneyland at Marne-la-Vallée, just outside Paris, on April 3, 1998, Rowe gave birth to Paris-Michael Katherine Jackson. As with Prince, Jackson took full responsibility for looking after his daughter.

OPPOSITE: *The poster for the ever-intriguing* Michael Jackson's Ghosts.
ABOVE: HIStory *in Amsterdam, at the end of the first European leg of the tour, September 1996.* FOLLOWING SPREAD: *Jackson ensured that* HIStory *would be his biggest tour to date; the onstage opulence and attention to detail was astounding.*

HIStory *saw one of the largest label-backed campaigns to rehabilitate an artist in recent times. The chutzpah surrounding it was extensive—hubristic even. It can be seen as the birth of celebrity as we know it today: all huge gesture and artifice. But succeed it did, selling in enormous quantities around the globe. It went some way to ameliorate the public furor that had exploded over what became known as "the Jordan Chandler case"—the single most damaging thing to happen to Jackson in his lifetime.*

CHAPTER 5

TALKIN', SQUEALIN', LYIN'?
JORDAN CHANDLER AND LISA MARIE PRESLEY

"If this is what I have to endure to prove my innocence, my complete innocence, so be it."

—MICHAEL JACKSON, DECEMBER 1993

Michael Jackson, famously having never had a childhood like you or I, had long been known for his desire to be around children, to provide him with inspiration and retain a purity in his life. As many had observed and biographer J. Randy Taraborrelli put into words, at this juncture, it was "known about as odd, but not necessarily inappropriate."[1] But when the accusations began to fly regarding Jordan Chandler, Michael Jackson became a damaged and vulnerable man.

As the *Dangerous* tour traversed the globe, Jackson befriended Jordan Chandler, the son of a dentist who worked in Los Angeles. Evan Chandler was known as the "dentist to the stars" and was a low-level Hollywood player, having written the screenplay for the Mel Brooks–directed Robin Hood spoof, *Men in Tights*. His ex-wife, Jordan's mother, June, had since married Dave Schwartz, the owner of a car rental business.

In May 1992, Jackson, in a rare moment of driving alone, had broken down on the L.A. freeway. Needing a car, he went into Schwartz's business. Knowing what a huge fan of Jackson his wife's son was, Schwartz told his mother to get down to the showroom and bring her boy. After the meeting, June—who loved Hollywood glamour—suggested that Jackson should call her son again; numbers were exchanged. It was to be the start of an obsession. Chandler came down to one of Jackson's hideouts in Century City, which had its own amusement arcade, and the two became friends.

OPPOSITE: *Not a stranger in Moscow after all—performing in Russia's capital, 1993.*

For the remainder of 1992, Jackson was to call Chandler weekly as the *Dangerous* tour continued. When he returned to L.A. in early 1993, the Chandler family—Jordan, his sister Lily, and his mother June—began to travel everywhere with Jackson, with Jackson increasingly imploring Jordan's mother to allow him to be alone with the child.

Though deeply suspicious, she was starstruck and impressed by Jackson's largesse. She tacitly accepted the special friendship, having been guaranteed by Jackson that there was nothing untoward going on, even after she had gleaned from her son Jackson's special code that they were to say three times a day, in the hope it would come true. The code ran thus:

"1. No wenches, bitches, heifers, or hos. 2. Never give up on your bliss. 3. Live with me in Neverland forever. 4. No conditioning. 5. Never Grow Up. 6. Be better than best friends."[2]

It could be argued that this was the behavior of very close friends. Or children.

Evan Chandler was initially concerned about nothing more sinister than that Jackson might usurp his role as Jordan's father figure; when he heard that they were sleeping in the same bed, however, he was not happy in the slightest. When June, Jordan, and Lily accompanied Jackson to the World Music Awards in Monaco that year, Jackson was seen openly bouncing Chandler on his knee.

The friendship couldn't have been more explicit to the world. With the boy's mother and daughter by his side, Jackson had a new family. The *National Enquirer* picked up on it. However their relationship is viewed, Jackson was absolutely playing with fire. It is simply not the conventional behavior of any man, bar a father, to spend such time alone in hotel suites with an underage boy and then to flaunt the child on his lap in front of the world's press.

Evan Chandler was increasingly furious. Soon after, however, he met Jackson, and the two seemed to get along—until Jackson cooled toward him when he began to feel that he was being interrogated too much about his relationship with the boy. Evan looked to amend the custody agreement of his divorce with June in July 1993; he wished to forbid Jackson from seeing Jordan.

Annoyed that Jackson was not returning his calls (he had aspirations that Jackson could further his career) and worried about his son, Evan then realized—in a conversation that was taped by June's husband, Dave Schwartz—that he could make money out of Jackson. "If I go through with this, I will get everything I want," he told Schwartz. "This man . . . is going to be humiliated beyond belief . . . he will not sell one more record." Evan had a client, fearsome showbusiness attorney Barry Rothman, who agreed to trade services with him to assist, as Taraborrelli notes, "dental for legal."[3]

The matter was further exacerbated when Jackson requested that Jordan accompany him on the final leg of the *Dangerous* tour, which was to start in late August that year. On August 2, while performing a dental procedure on his son using the relaxant drug sodium amytal, Evan questioned Jordan and concluded than Jackson had touched him intimately. Evan went to see Jackson and confronted him. After Jackson denied everything, he received a letter sent via his attorney, demanding $20 million; instead, Jackson offered Chandler a three-film script development deal, each at $350,000, with the promise of having a major film house review the scripts. Chandler declined the offer. He didn't want to get his son back to his ex-wife, either, as she would allow the relationship to continue.

June Chandler was now effectively being denied access to her son by her ex-husband. She wanted her son back, and a court date was set to look again at custody rights of the child. With negotiations with Jackson stalled, Evan took his son to a psychiatrist, Dr. Mathis Abrams. Here, Jordan allegedly confessed to a sexual relationship with Jackson. Abrams reported his findings to the Los Angeles County Department of Children's Services and the LAPD. Jordan said the same things to the police, although June and Dave Schwartz later said they felt it was likely that Jordan could well have been manipulated by his father.

On August 24, it was announced that Michael Jackson was under investigation by the Los Angeles Police Department for allegations of child molestation against Jordan Chandler. It became a huge field day for an America fast getting used to twenty-four-hour news reporting, having witnessed every bullet in the first Gulf War and every nuance of the Rodney King case on television. This was truly shocking: the nation's biggest idol was in trouble, confirming everyone's worst suspicion that he was more than just eccentric. Less than a decade ago, he was being lauded by President Reagan; now, as Nelson George writes, "Chandler, then

Jackson and Jordan Chandler at the World Music Awards, Monaco, May 1993.

ABOVE: *Aerial view of Jackson's beloved Neverland Ranch.* OPPOSITE: *Taking his message out across the world: Jackson in Thailand toward the end of the* Dangerous *tour, August 1993.*

a Beverly Hills dentist, would forever change Michael's public image (much more so in the United States than overseas) and cast a sinister shadow on his eccentricities past (Bubbles the chimp, the Elephant Man's bones) and future (brief marriages to Priscilla Presley and Debbie Rowe, covering his children's heads in blankets and veils in public)."[4]

It was an *enormous* hot potato. The police moved in and searched Neverland, yet nothing deeply incriminating was found. There were

supposedly books of undressed boys that Jackson was unaware of; he suggested that fans had sent them. As the days progressed, it became apparent that Evan Chandler owed $68,000 in child-support payments, so perhaps there was an ulterior motive at play . . .

NO LONGER DANGEROUS

As the final leg of his *Dangerous* tour started in Thailand, Jackson's media advisor, Anthony

Sibling adoration: Michael with his sister Janet at the 35th Grammy Awards, 1993.

Pellicano, offered to the world's press two other boys who had slept in Jackson's bed. Although he intended to show that Jackson was not a threat to children, it somewhat strengthened the case against him.

The details of the case were paraded in a wholly biased-against-Jackson manner by the gaudier end of the press. Then, Jackson's estranged sister LaToya issued a statement, breaking away from the rest of the family's silence and suggesting that her brother was, indeed, guilty. "If he was any other thirty-five-year old man who was sleeping with little boys, you wouldn't like this guy."[5]

On November 11, 2003, Jackson performed his final show at El Estadio del Azteca in Mexico City; the rest of the *Dangerous* tour was canceled. His hotel room was in shambles, and there was evidence of drug abuse. He was flown to London and whisked into the Charter Nightingale Clinic in Chelsea. The next day, he announced why the tour had been curtailed: he was an addict and he needed help. Jackson announced to the world that he had begun taking painkillers in 1984, after the Pepsi accident, but was now dependent on Ativan, Valium, and Xanax as a result of Chandler's allegations.

In December, Jackson was subjected to a humiliating series of naked police photographs, taken to ascertain if his body markings matched with Chandler's descriptions of him. Santa Barbara District Attorney Thomas Sneddon was present. (Whether a match was proven has never been fully verified.) This process crippled Jackson mentally. Here he was the King of Pop, shamed into such a degrading ritual.

ABOVE: *"If this is what I have to endure to prove my innocence, my complete innocence, so be it."* **BELOW:** *Jackson performs with Stevie Wonder, Aretha Franklin, and Diana Ross at Bill Clinton's presidential inauguration, January 1993.*

On December 22, Jackson released a video statement from Neverland. Acknowledging that he had been through treatment for addiction to pain medication, he stressed his innocence and stated, "I have been forced to submit to a dehumanizing and humiliating examination. . . . It was the most humiliating ordeal of my life. . . . But if this is what I have to endure to prove my innocence, my complete innocence, so be it."

Superstars like Michael Jackson didn't have to endure such demeaning behavior, surely. A court case was slated for March 1994.

On January 25, 1994, the case was settled out of court for $22 million. Of that sum, $20 million went to Jordan, and $1 million each to his parents, with attorney Larry Feldman receiving around $5 million in contingency fees from all three. No charges were pressed against Jackson, with the authorities citing a lack of evidence.

Did the settlement show that, to Jackson, money could solve everything; that it was possible to pay off the parties for their silence? Was Jackson paying money to keep the suspects quiet, or was there simply nothing there? Jackson told biographer J. Randy Taraborelli that "too much damage had already been done to everyone involved. I don't care what people think. I know the truth. If anyone has ever gone through something like this, they'd know you'd do anything to end it." Taraborrelli, a long-term friend, asked Jackson if he thought the payment would suggest to the wider public he was indeed guilty. According to Taraborelli, Jackson's reply was, "It's my talent. My hard work. My life. My decision."[6]

Later, Jackson was asked by Diane Sawyer, on ABC's *Primetime*, "Did you ever fondle this or any other child?"

"I could never harm a child," Jackson replied. "It's not in my heart, it's not who I am . . . I'm not even interested in that."

When asked his view on those who do harm to children, Jackson said, "I think they need help in some kind of way," before stating, "Nothing . . . matched me to those charges." Following on from what he said to Taraborrelli, he added, "I talked to my lawyers . . . can [you] guarantee my justice can prevail," before he realized, "I have got to do something to get out from this nightmare. The idea just isn't fair . . . there wasn't one piece of information that says I did that."

POP KING MARRIES ROCK 'N' ROLL PRINCESS

On May 26, 1994, suddenly, in a flash, Michael Jackson married Lisa Marie Presley, the only daughter of the King of Rock 'n' Roll, Elvis Presley. It was little over four months since the resolution of the Chandler case, and it all seemed rather incredible.

Concurrently with the Chandler affair, Jackson had become reacquainted with Presley, whom he had first met as a six-year-old when she saw his shows in Las Vegas in 1974. They'd met again through his lawyer, John Branca; Jackson would call Lisa frequently from his hotel room on the *Dangerous* tour. He liked her because she seemed to understand him. Realizing that she was separated from her husband, Danny Keough,

OPPOSITE: *In Versailles with Lisa Marie Presley, 1994.*

Jackson knew he liked her so much that he proposed to her on the telephone.

"If I asked you to marry me, would you do it?" he asked. She replied that she would.

They had been dating for a period of time, yet somehow it didn't get into the press. It was hidden in plain sight. With all of Jackson's unusual and stellar friendships, why should Presley be any different from, say, Liza Minnelli? The couple married on May 26, in the Dominican Republic. When the news was made public in July, opinions about the relationship ranged, as Diane Sawyer pointed out on ABC's *Primetime Live* in 1995, from "astonishment to delight to suspicion—it was all too convenient."

Lisa Marie Presley issued a statement to the world's press: "My married name is Mrs. Lisa Marie Presley-Jackson. My marriage to Michael Jackson took place in a private ceremony outside the United States weeks ago. It was not formally announced until now for several reasons; foremost being that we are both very private people living in the glare of the public media. We both wanted a private marriage ceremony without the distraction of a media circus. I am very much in love with Michael; I dedicate my life to being his wife. I understand and support him. We both look forward to raising a family and living happy, healthy lives together. We hope friends and fans will understand and respect our privacy."[7] It certainly put Jackson back on the front pages for something other than the Chandler case.

"I was in touch with him during the charges, talking when he disappeared; I was part of the whole thing," Lisa Marie later said. One thing is for sure: she knew what it was like to be around one of the biggest and most eccentric stars in the world.

The two made their first public appearance together at the MTV Video Music Awards at Radio City Music Hall in New York on September 8. They received a spontaneous and prolonged standing ovation. Reflecting on their four months of marriage, Jackson quipped, "And to think, nobody thought this would last." The two kissed passionately before leaving the stage.

It was to be a fiery relationship: Lisa Marie Presley made it plain in later life that they were very much a couple. "I am going to say now what I have never said before, because I want the truth out there for once," she said in 2009. "Our relationship was not 'a sham,' as is being reported in the press. It was an unusual relationship, yes, where two unusual people who did not live or know a 'normal life' found a connection, perhaps with some suspect timing on his part. Nonetheless, I do believe he loved me as much as he could love anyone and I loved him very much."

Lisa Marie Presley wanted to look after Michael, to "save him," as she later stated. "His family and his loved ones also wanted to save him from this as well," she added, "but didn't know how . . . in trying to save him, I almost lost myself."[8]

For the next year, they were inseparable.

OPPOSITE: *Jackson onstage with Lisa Marie at the MTV Video Music Awards in 1994.*

If he had known what lay ahead of him, Jackson may have concentrated more on his time in the studio—the place where he truly came alive. The work on Dangerous *was extensive and, in many respects, groundbreaking. Since the release of* Bad, *hip-hop and swingbeat had come to dominate African-American pop. In making* Dangerous, *his first album away from Quincy Jones in a decade and a half, Jackson sought to place himself on the leading edge.*

CHAPTER 6

I AM TIRED OF THIS BUSINESS

DANGEROUS

———————

"What is lacked in tunefulness is gained in precision-machined grooves of industrial strength."

—MAT SNOW, Q MAGAZINE[1]

"WACKO JACKO"

It has been said that in order to keep the press at bay, Jackson was party to constructing his "Wacko Jacko" character. Like other well-known pop eccentrics, he felt it was good for business: feeding the press machine while enabling an artist discreetly to continue with his own life. What had become interesting tics were now becoming major characteristics, and tales rose from the Jackson camp like smoke from a bonfire on a fall evening.

"In every sense of the word, Michael was bad," former CBS Records president Walter Yetnikoff writes in his autobiography, *Howling at the Moon.* "As I watched him change over the next five or six years, I was alternately impressed and alarmed. His artistic brilliance stood in contrast to his personal behavior. He grew more isolated, evolving from strange to weird to outrageously (and perhaps calculatingly) bizarre."[2]

As news media gave way to entertainment media and rolling news, there was a lot of space to fill. Jackson began to change his appearance. Whether it was "skin bleaching" or the skin-lightening disease vitiligo, Michael Jackson began to get whiter, which fueled all manner of speculation that he was trying to leave his roots to increase his worldwide appeal. As Caroline Sullivan of the *Guardian* was later to note, "As his appearance changed, rumors about his lifestyle proliferated. Jackson supposedly slept in an oxygen tent, clothed Bubbles in matching outfits, and offered to buy the Elephant Man's bones. He began to appear in public wearing a surgical mask, and seemed to be asexual, with no significant relationships during his twenties."[3]

OPPOSITE: *The King and Queen step out: Jackon and Madonna at an Academy Awards after-party, Spago, Los Angeles, 1991.*

During this period, there was one interestingly dissenting voice. "I am seriously concerned about the state of Michael Jackson's mental health," Tom Graves wrote in *Rock & Roll Disc* magazine in 1987. "The news items grow more bizarre by the week and Michael seems to be receding deeper into that Sleeping Beauty's castle of his mind. It is obvious he is going through one king-hell identity crisis." Questioning the need for all the cosmetic changes that left Jackson looking "whiter and more feminine," Graves suggested it was time to stop "carping and snickering" and speak out about what was going on. "I'm calling on those whom Michael Jackson trusts . . . to encourage him to seek professional help. He desperately needs someone to bring him back to reality. We don't need another slow death like Elvis or Brian Wilson."[4] Graves' was a curious, questioning voice that stood alone from both the mass adulation or wholesale ridicule that Jackson was subject to.

DANGER LIES AHEAD

It was time for Michael Jackson to return to work. The *Bad* tour had been everything that he'd wanted it to be, but he knew that his next album would need to be something special indeed. His pride had been knocked by what was in his and no one else's eyes the relative failure of *Bad* in selling twenty million units compared with *Thriller*'s forty million.

There were rumors that Jackson had ended his near decade-long collaboration with Quincy Jones. In March 1990, Jones told *Rhythm and News* magazine, "I don't know if there will be another collaboration with us. We worked together for ten years. I'm headed toward another direction. I think Michael really should do his own thing now."[5] If he was to work without Jones, Jackson's new album would need to be doubly special.

In what would be a recurring theme, Epic, now owned by Sony, asked Jackson if he would be interested in releasing a new greatest-hits LP for the 1990 Christmas market, with the possibility of adding four new tracks amid some outtakes. The project was tentatively titled *Decade*, but Jackson eschewed the idea and instead began recording a new album with producers such as Bill Bottrell, L.A. Reid, and Babyface.

Excited by the prospect of a new album, and aware of the potency of its artist, in March 1991, Sony signed a new deal with Jackson for a reported $50 million. At the time, this was the most lucrative deal in music history, with the percentage per album sold due to Jackson in the region of 25 percent.

Recording sessions for his forthcoming album, which was to become known as *Dangerous*, took place at Record One's Studio Two and Ocean Way in Los Angeles, starting in June 1990, and ended at both Larrabee North and Ocean Way Studios on October 29, 1991. Spanning sixteen months, this was the most extensive recording project of Jackson's career at the time. Never before had he been under quite such scrutiny.

Swingbeat guru Teddy Riley was to be Jackson's principal choice as producer, although as Nelson George writes, while it looked as though Jackson had chosen Riley "as his new muse . . . in truth, he replaced Quincy with himself. Even though Teddy would produce

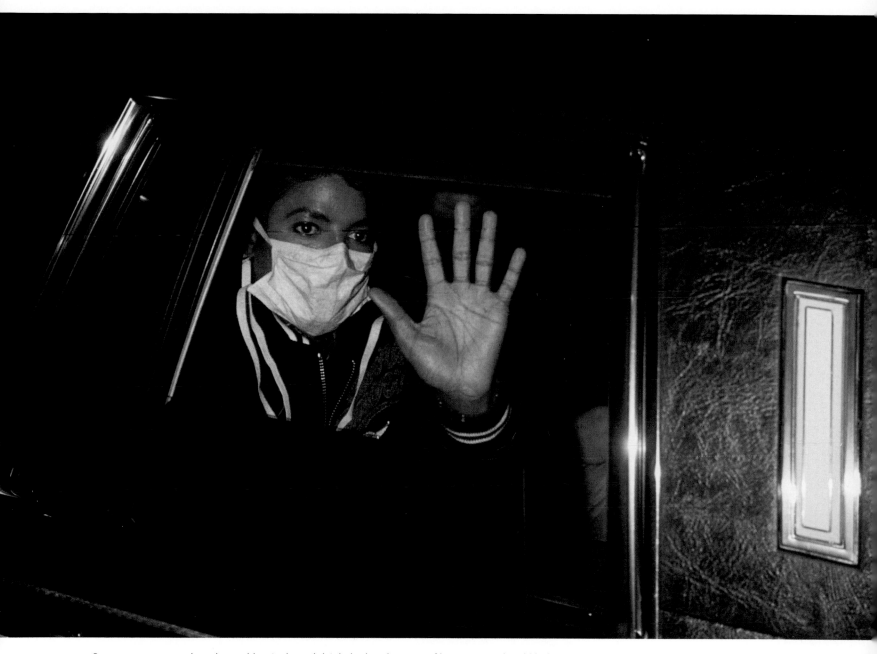

By wearing a surgical mask in public, Jackson didn't help dispel rumors of his increasingly odd behavior.

most of *Dangerous* and contribute to much of Michael's recorded output over the course of his final albums, Michael worked with a wide range of producer/writers, often in search of dance floor credibility and contemporary sounds."[6]

Compared with the focus of *Thriller* and even *Bad*, the sessions for *Dangerous* were sprawling. Teddy Riley moved to California to be on permanent call for Michael, and his family moved out, too. Jackson effectively forbade them to leave the area. Riley recalled to Nelson George that during one session, Jackson had to pop out; thinking he'd gone to do some local business, he kept the microphone ready for his next vocal. Riley later received a call to say that Jackson had gone to Australia, and would be back in a fortnight.

Whether or not *Dangerous* has stood the test of time as well as the albums that went before it is ripe for conjecture; what is definitely true is that, at the time, *Dangerous*, more so than *Bad*, was something of a template for how music was going to sound for the rest of the decade/century.

BLACK OR WHITE?

Every new album needs its lead single—the calling card that begins the campaign. After the relative red herrings of both "The Girl Is Mine" and "I Just Can't Stop Loving You" last time around, this time nothing would be left to chance. "Black or White" took the rock/dance hybrid that Jackson had practically single-handedly invented on "Beat It," and then upped the game. It defined the next phase of Michael Jackson. With its route-one guitar riff—with Slash as featured guitarist on the intro—and singsong chorus, there is something sweetly and deceptively stupid about it all.

Released in November 1991, the single soon shot to No. 1 on both sides of the Atlantic, accompanied by a typically lengthy video starring white-hot child actor Macaulay Culkin. It also introduced Jackson's new long, long black hair, white vest, and strapped-up arms. The other completely unavoidable matter was the color of his skin. This was the first time Jackson had paraded his vitiligo so publicly. As well as being a plea for racial harmony, the record was an immediate call to his detractors: what did it matter if he was black or white?

DANGEROUS

With "Black or White" selling strongly worldwide, it was time for the album: the sprawling, commercial, curious, and sonically adventurous *Dangerous*. The album also furthered Jackson's *Bad* stance of paranoia and fear, of the world closing in on him, alongside glorious paeans for world unity.

The album opens with one of his greatest cuts. "Jam" can be heard as a distant cousin of

OPPOSITE: *Teddy Riley—his productions made Jackson's work more contemporary for urban America.* ABOVE: *Michael Jackson and Slash performing "Black or White," November 1991.*

the three big anthems that had opened the Jones trilogy: "Don't Stop 'til You Get Enough," "Wanna Be Startin' Somethin'," and "Bad." And with this huge atonal starter as an album fanfare, it set the template for the rest of his career. "Jam" sounds like one long plea. Over Riley's mechanical beats, Jackson sets out his stall; Heavy D. acts as the MC of the day, bringing in some street flavor. *Q* magazine said at the time that "Jam" was "as exciting as a record which appears to have dispensed altogether with any notion of melody can possibly be (four people are credited with writing the music)."[7] It is one of the most important songs in Jackson's catalogue; with Jackson spitting out his words in short bursts, he effectively sets the template for '90s R&B. It might be the last time he held such sway. As Nelson George states, "Michael spews words across the track like an AK-47 assault rifle, a ferociously controlled vocal that is as close to rapping as a singer can come."[8]

One of the song's four writers was long-term collaborator Bruce Swedien. "It was no accident that 'Jam' was such a huge song," he told me in 2009. "I wrote it with René Moore; we had this idea of looping high-energy drum tracks. Michael got really involved and we took it to the sky. It gives me chills thinking about those sessions. Michael and I had a saying when we were recording *Dangerous*—'the quality goes in before the name goes on'—and we believed that."[9]

"Jam" was released as the fourth single from the album, after "Black or White," "Remember the Time" (a slice of thoroughly beguiling new jack swing written with Riley and Bernard Belle), and "In the Closet." A short film directed by John Singleton accompanied the track, set in ancient Egypt and featuring stars such as Iman, Eddie Murphy, and Magic Johnson. The intro to "Why You Wanna Trip on Me" can now be seen almost as a test case for the latest studio technology, as can the aggressive, scything beats on "In the Closet"; both open out into choruses to die for. To illustrate the circles in which Jackson was now moving, "In the Closet" includes a spoken-word section by Princess Stephanie of Monaco. Its call for whatever two people do or say to each other to be kept "in the closet" could later be perceived as carrying deeper meanings.

Elsewhere, the album offers an almost endless stream of pop and soul anthems: "Heal the World" is built on "We Are the World," a tender plea for the eradication of world poverty. The gospel-influenced "Will You Be There" opens with a section of Beethoven's "Ode to Joy" played by the Cleveland Orchestra; it is grandiose but able to just stay on the right side of being over the top throughout. The cover of "Gone Too Soon" by Larry Grossman and Buz Kohan was included for the memory of Ryan White, a teenager from Indiana who was expelled from school for having HIV/AIDS; "Who Is It" is a fantastic R&B number, while "Give In to Me" is the album's brooding rock track.

Dangerous is an album of enormous excess. The period running into it would be the last one of little complication for Jackson. There was no real scandal beyond the "Wacko Jacko" nature of it all. With its intricate sleeve, illustrated by American painter Mark Ryden, full of meaning-heavy clues, *Dangerous* was released at the end of 1991, and it took up residence at the top of the world's album charts that Christmas. It went on to sell thirty-two million copies worldwide and around the globe: nine of its fourteen tracks were taken as singles.

Dangerous received a mixed but mainly positive reaction from the press, but truly speaking, at this point, it mattered little what they said; this was a brand-new Michael Jackson. For *Q* magazine, "The 77-minute span of *Dangerous* encompasses the entire range of what has come to be expected from Michael Jackson: aggression and schmaltz, paranoia and rose-tinted optimism, godliness and megalomania, innovation and caution, the sublime and the ridiculous. Foremost, however, it offers danceability to an alarmingly intense degree."[10]

THE DANGEROUS TOUR

Now here was a spectacle. Jackson had to top the *Bad* tour. The sixteen-month-long *Dangerous* tour was arduous and complex. It began in Munich, at the Olympic Stadium, on June 27, 1992, and featured eighteen numbers from across his career, and an ending that was groundbreaking: overseen by magician David Copperfield, it culminated with Jackson dressing as an astronaut, strapping on a jetpack, and propelling himself out of the stadium. That it was, of course, a stunt double (Kinnie Gibson) mattered not a jot—this was the world-class entertainment people expected from the King of Pop, and as this was now officially his title, he needed to act even more like one. The show was a military operation with Jackson in the middle, wearing his army jackets—and even utilizing the army itself at a show in Bucharest.

"I Just Can't Stop Loving You" vocalist (and "Man in the Mirror" co-writer) Siedah Garrett joined Jackson on the road. As she recalled in 2013, "Michael was a perfectionist, and very detail-oriented. He insisted on giving his fans exactly what they heard on the album, and more. However, for his band members, we would grow a little weary of doing the exact same thing every night. During one show, I decided to surprise

The jetpack finale at the Dangerous *concerts remains one of the greatest pop spectacles of all time.*

OPPOSITE AND ABOVE: *The* Dangerous *tour was bigger and more audacious than anything Jackson had staged to date.*

Michael by appearing onstage wearing a blond wig to sing our duet. Michael was initially taken aback, but then was amused, and couldn't stop laughing onstage."[11]

On January 31, 1993, Jackson again set a precedent when he ushered in a new age of half-time performances at Super Bowl XXVII at the Rose Bowl in Pasadena, California. Previously, the shows had featured marching bands or aging performers respectfully singing the hits of yesteryear; here, Jackson brought a scaled-down version of the *Dangerous* tour to the interval, decanting "Jam," "Billie Jean," "Black or White," "We Are the World," and "Heal the World" into a twelve-minute set. It even had the tricksy opening of the *Dangerous* tour, with Jackson more-or-less catapulted onto the stage.

For "Heal the World," 3,500 children joined Jackson onstage, and there was an enormous flashcard stunt to promote Jackson's new Heal the World foundation. As a result, the ratings

OPPOSITE: *Jackson ushered in a new era of halftime performances at The Super Bowl.* TOP: *Three of the most important people in Jackson's life in the early '90s: Antonio "L.A." Reid, Brooke Shields, and Kenneth Edmonds, aka Babyface.* ABOVE: *His Super Bowl finale was comprised of 3,500 children singing "Heal The World."*

OPPOSITE: *With Brooke Shields, post–Grammy Awards, 1993.* ABOVE: *Hanging with his confidant Liz Taylor, summer 1992.*

for the football game shot through the roof—an estimated 120 million people watched the halftime show—and set the template for all future performances, which would become grander and grander, and feature acts such as the Who, Paul McCartney, Phil Collins, Madonna, and Michael's sister Janet.

On February 10, 1993, Michael Jackson spoke with Oprah Winfrey on American national television. He gave her a tour of Neverland and discussed his vitiligo, nose surgery, and love life. Jackson's appearance was changing radically. "It is something I cannot help," he said. "When people make up stories that I don't want to be who I am, it hurts me. It's a problem for me. I

can't control it. But what about all the millions of people who sit in the sun to become darker, to become other than what they are? Nobody says nothing about that."[12]

He spoke, too, about his girlfriend, Brooke Shields. Elizabeth Taylor appeared and told the world that Jackson was the "least weird man she had ever known." It was a complete charm offensive. The show gained ninety million viewers and was, at the time, the fourth most-watched program in the history of US television. It would be the last time Jackson would gain such an enormous audience on his own soil for the right reasons. It had all seemed much simpler when he had the world at his feet.

Dangerous had shown what Michael Jackson—the artist and showman—could achieve when defending his title as the world's No. 1. It was a spirited performance, made by a performer who knew exactly what he had to do to maintain his pop supremacy in a fast-moving world. Scrolling back to before then, Bad, released in 1987, was a very different album. Jackson's last with Quincy Jones, it saw him go out all-guns blazing, bankrolled by the obvious and excited enthusiasm of Sony, to top Thriller.

CHAPTER 7

THE WHOLE WORLD HAS TO ANSWER RIGHT NOW

BAD

"I write the songs and do the music and then Quincy brings out the best in me."

—MICHAEL JACKSON, 1988[1]

What do you do when you are right up there at the top? Release an album that is rather remarkable, and of the same standard as the last, and offer a selection of hit singles so ripe that nobody could complain. Except that, whatever happened, *Bad* was not *Thriller*, and nor it ever could be. *Thriller* already felt something like a museum piece, being five years old. The pretty young man on the cover seemed to come from another era. So much water had flowed under the bridge. The twenty-nine-year-old on the cover of *Bad* was dolled up to the nines in his street gear, and he meant business.

BAD TIMES AHEAD

Bad is such a fascinating subject, the album recorded in the eye of the storm, at the zenith of Michael Jackson's popularity. The genesis of the title allegedly arose from a conversation between Jackson and Columbia president Walter Yetnikoff. Jackson was hiding behind his record company as he wished to veto a release by his brother Jermaine. When Yetnikoff suggested that it would make *him* the bad guy instead of Michael, Jackson replied, "That's a great idea for the title of my next solo album."[2]

The last time Jackson had been heard on album was in his relative cameos on his brothers' *Victory* album. On a positive note, spending time on that record spared him from having to release his own album, which could have

OPPOSITE: *By the late 1980s, Jackson had reached the zenith of his celebrity, and often hid behind an array of scarves and masks.*

WE ARE HERE TO CHANGE THE WORLD.

GEORGE LUCAS presents A 3-D MUSICAL MOTION PICTURE SPACE ADVENTURE.
Directed by FRANCIS COPPOLA starring MICHAEL JACKSON as CAPTAIN EO
PRESENTED BY THE EASTMAN KODAK COMPANY AT DISNEYLAND AND
WALT DISNEY WORLD EPCOT CENTER... AND NOWHERE ELSE IN THE UNIVERSE!

dated as badly as most records from 1984–1985, with their clunky drum machines and over-obvious synthesizers. The leap from the smooth early-'80s-ness of *Thriller* to the sound of *Bad* was remarkable.

There were, as we know, various projects that Jackson was involved with since "We Are the World," such as *Captain EO*, a seventeen-minute 3-D film of pure fantasy that took Jackson even further out to be with his fans. Directed by Francis Ford Coppola, this piece of science-fiction hokum was made to be shown at Disney theme parks. It was, in fact, the first "4-D" film, as the screenings made use of in-theater effects such as smoke and lasers. Co-starring Anjelica Huston, the film was notable for featuring two new Jackson originals: the upbeat sketch "We Are Here to Change the World" (which Deniece Williams would later cover) and the first version of a track that would make it to *Bad*, "Another Part of Me." It was also at this time that tales of Jackson sleeping in a hyperbaric chamber surfaced—the thirst for news and information about him seemed simply unquenchable.

ABOVE: *The film poster for Captain EO; it was a huge success at the theme parks where it was played.*
RIGHT: *Aye, aye, Captain: working on Captain EO with Francis Ford Coppola and George Lucas.* OPPOSITE: *The four-dimensional Michael Jackson: Captain EO.*

MAKING BAD

Quincy Jones knew exactly what he was doing. Recorded at Westlake Studios in a seven-month burst from the start of January 1987, *Bad* was a fabulous workshop of machine-tooled sounds with a big, beating heart. This time, Rod Temperton was off the scene, and the album was packed with Jackson originals, with just two outside songs among the ten tracks.

The recording of *Bad* saw the whole Michael Jackson zoo in full effect. And, in this instance, it *was* an actual zoo. "Bubbles was in the studio with us," engineer Bruce Swedien said. Ah yes, Bubbles, Jackson's famous chimpanzee. "He was a juvenile delinquent, though. When he'd get out of line, Michael would take off his black loafer and whap him on the head to shape him up a little. He would be up in the control room with us with his trainer Bob Hughes. After a while when we'd all had enough of Bubbles, Michael would send him home." And if the chimp weren't enough, the snake would be there, too. "The boa, Muscles, was with us during *Bad* as well. Quincy was absolutely terrified of snakes . . . we let him crawl

all over the control console and he could not bump a button. He liked it because it was warm. He was everywhere."[3]

It was clear, however, that there was some tension between Quincy Jones and Jackson. As Jackson notes in *Moonwalk*, "I write the songs and do the music and then Quincy brings out the best in me. . . . If we struggle at all, it's about new stuff, the latest technology."[4]

Jackson's desire to remain at the leading edge meant that he needed the latest in sonics, audio and studio development, and players. Between them, Jones and Jackson again got the very best players: Nathan East, Greg Phillinganes, and John Robinson all returned; to emphasize the links between past and present, Hammond legend Jimmy Smith appears on the street-influenced title track. This ability to juxtapose was one of Jones' greatest tricks. As critic Mat Snow noted, "*Bad* jazz organist Jimmy Smith was producer Quincy Jones' way of humanizing the chip-generated rhythm."[5]

The album starts at fever pitch and hardly gives the listener a minute to rest. Every high and low has been sculpted for maximum effect. "Another Part of Me," now fleshed out from the *Captain EO* version, is smooth urban soul; "The Way You Make Me Feel" glistening R&B; "Dirty Diana" (with Billy Idol's guitarist Steve Stevens doing an Eddie Van Halen) and "Smooth Criminal," with its repetitive chorus and rocky propulsion, would cover off the rock fans. "Liberian Girl" is a touchingly sweet ballad. "The Way You Make Me Feel" is irresistible, a pure slice of Motown pop updated with the clunks and whirrs of the day.

"Man in the Mirror" was written by Siedah Garrett and Glenn Ballard. Garrett had been

OPPOSITE: *Jackson and "juvenile delinquent" Bubbles in Japan, September 1987.* ABOVE: *With its Steve Stevens guitar solo, "Dirty Diana" became the fifth and final US No.1 single from* Bad.

instructed by Jones to provide a final song for the album. "We need another smash for Michael's album," he told her. "I just want hits, that's all I want."[6] Garrett didn't want just to give Jackson another "baby I love you" song; instead, she came up with one of the most anthemic songs in Jackson's career. Jones told her that it was one of the best songs that he had heard in ten years; with its message of personal empowerment (then still a relatively new concept) and its later video of icons for peace and change, it was a remarkable song, and one with which Jackson would become inseparable.

Garrett also appears on the album's lead single, "I Just Can't Stop Loving You." Both Whitney Houston and Barbra Streisand had been mooted to perform vocal duties, but in the end the role fell to Garrett, who had been working with Jones and had made such an impression on Dennis Edwards' "Don't Look

ABOVE: *Recording "I Just Can't Stop Loving You" with Siedah Garrett, 1987.* OPPOSITE: *"Man in the Mirror" remained one of Jackson's favorite songs.*

Any Further" in 1984. It would be one of only two duets that Michael performed with females (the other being his partnership with sister Janet on "Scream").

"I Just Can't Stop Loving You" offers respite compared to the other material, with live musicians playing the parts. (It is the only track on the album to feature a live, not synthesized, bass guitar, for example.) It is telling also that there was no video for this song, almost like it was to remain some kind of secret, allowing listeners to project their own romances on to the music. Garrett offers a sweet counterpart to Jackson, although her role was made difficult in the studio by him throwing popcorn in her face each time she tried to record the vocal. As *Rolling Stone* asked,

"Who, having heard the song at least twice, can fail to remember that chorus?"[7] It was a beautiful, uplifting, heartfelt number.

Of the songs on *Bad*, it is only the Stevie Wonder duet "Just Good Friends" that promises so much yet delivers so little; it's one of those numbers that, every time you hear it, it's like you've never heard it before, and not in a good way. "Speed Demon" is something of a red herring: the first genuinely pointless track on a Michael Jackson album since Motown days. It takes the machine groove right down to the metal, while as the UK paper *NME* stated, "Lyrically, Michael plays the familiar paranoid he first became on 'This Place Hotel'—'Look in the view mirror/Is he hot on my tracks?'"[8]

BREAKING BAD

Trailed by the worldwide No. 1 "I Just Can't Stop Loving You," *Bad* was released on August 31, 1987. The anticipation was palpable, but as it shot to the summit of the world's listings, the overall view from the critics was one of some indifference.

In the United States, Tom Graves wrote in *Rock & Roll Record*, "On all but a couple of the tracks on *Thriller*, the music was like an aural equivalent of that granulated candy that pops and tingles when placed on the tongue. On *Bad* only the title track and a few others reach that level of stunning."[9] *Rolling Stone* opined, "If these songs—even 'Smooth Criminal,' with its incessant 'Annie, are you okay?'—seem less threatening than previous dream songs, like 'Heartbreak Hotel' and 'Wanna Be Startin' Somethin',' it's because Jackson's perspective has changed. He is no longer the victim, the

vegetable they want to eat up, but a concerned observer or a participant with power."[10]

In the UK, Richard Cook of *Sounds* wrote, "The looseness and swing of all 'traditional' black musics are entirely absent. It's the highest tribute to Michael Jackson's genius that he instills as much humanity into *Bad* as he does."[11] The *NME* said, "*Bad* shows Michael Jackson aloof from what's going on, yet superbly in control. Alone in the womb of the studio, he sings to himself, the best, most attentive audience he will ever have . . . *Bad* isn't an answer record to anybody; it makes no attempt to be a maverick montage, like a Prince album. The songs are all showpieces, rather than fragments of a point of view. They reveal little of what is on this lonely man's mind."[12]

It mattered not what the critics thought. With Frank DiLeo looking after Michael, Epic (and, as the album's sales path progressed, Sony, which had bought Epic) putting its full marketing muscle behind it, and Jackson undertaking his first solo world tour, the *Bad* campaign had truly begun.

It was clear that the videos would need to

ABOVE: *The men behind the mirror: producer Quincy Jones and manager Frank DiLeo, 1988.* OPPOSITE: *Sharing the stage with the yet-to-be-famous-in-her-own-right Sheryl Crow, Wembley Stadium, July 1988.*

be something else for this album. Venerated film director Martin Scorsese was drafted in to direct one for the album's title track. An epic shoot, it emulated the "Beat It" video, casting Jackson as a gang leader and setting the elaborate dance routines on the New York subway. Scorsese later dissected the making of the "Bad" promo (or "short film," as we would learn Jackson wished his videos to be called) with his editor Thelma Schoonmaker for Spike Lee's documentary on the making of the album. Scorsese recalled taking Jackson to a brownstone and Jackson incredulously asking him, "Do people live here?"

On watching the video, you forget how, in the wake of hip-hop, Jackson was trying to reconnect to the street. Scorsese was gobsmacked when he encountered Jackson's first crotch-grab.

BAD TOUR

Although *Bad* did not fulfill Jackson's wish of selling one hundred million units, it was not for want of trying. *Bad* spawned five US No. 1s and nine Top 10 singles. Spike Lee later argued that *Bad* was black music's first stadium album, and boy, did Jackson work it.

Jackson had long regretted that he had not toured *Thriller*. *Bad* would need to be taken out to the masses, and people now would be expecting something on an unparalleled scale. It was time to see Jackson the solo artist, not surrounded by his brothers. Sponsored by Pepsi, the tour would ultimately include 123 concerts in fifteen countries. Jackson would play to over four million people. The first leg began in Japan on September 12, 1987, and ran through to the end of November, before restarting in February the following year in North America, taking in Europe and returning to Japan before ultimately finishing in L.A. in January 1989.

This was a gold-standard show, with costumes designed by Gianni Versace and a band including long-term associate Greg Phillinganes as music director and the then-unknown Sheryl Crow on backing vocals (and also taking the Siedah Garrett role on "I Just Can't Stop Loving You"). The set covered off his Jackson years with a medley, before focusing on his last three groundbreaking albums.

In London, Jackson played Wembley Stadium for seven sold-out concerts; the July 16 show was attended by Prince Charles and Diana, Princess of Wales, with whom Jackson would develop a friendship. In Cork, Ireland, there was a warm welcome and mass hysteria. The response in Japan was so great that the tour returned there for a second leg. All the while, singles were being released to extend the lifecycle of the album. It was one of the biggest tours of all time and was entered into the *Guinness Book of World Records* for playing to the most people ever at that point.

TOP: *Jackson's series of concerts at London's Wembley Stadium was one of the undisputed highlights of the Bad tour.* LEFT: *Jackson's superstardom was such that royalty would present his awards to him: Princess Diana, backstage at Wembley.* OPPOSITE: *Buckled up at the Hartford Civic Center, Connecticut, March 1988.*

MOONWALK, NEVERLAND, AND MOONWALKER

With the tour underway and the album in the world's charts, Jackson brought out his autobiography, *Moonwalk*. Published by Doubleday, the book was rather remarkably edited by Jacqueline Kennedy Onassis, who also wrote a brief introduction. It was originally going to be ghostwritten, until Jackson decided to write it himself. It was, of course, a publishing sensation, racing to the top of the *New York Times* best-seller list. A light but compelling read, in it Jackson writes about his father's temper and strictness, his plastic surgery, his diet, and his image. "I think I have a goody-goody image

OPPOSITE: *On the set of the "Bad" video, which was directed by Martin Scorsese and filmed in the Hoyt-Schermerhorn subway station in Brooklyn, New York.* RIGHT: *Just another chart to top:* Moonwalk *headed up all best-seller lists when it became the publishing phenomenon of 1988.* BELOW: *Jackson performing at the Grammy Awards, 1998.*

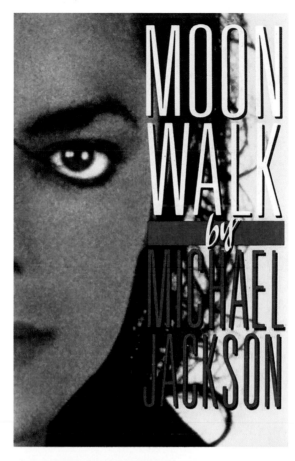

ABOVE: *A still from the Jim Blashfield-directed "Leave Me Alone" video.* OPPOSITE: *At the end of the Speed Demon sequence in* Moonwalker, *Jackson is pulled over by a cop for performing in a "No Dancing Zone." He had just been dancing with Claymation rabbit Spike.*

in the press and I hate that, but it's hard to fight because I don't normally talk about myself," he writes. "I am a shy person . . . When Doubleday approached me about doing this book, I was interested in being able to talk about how I feel in a book that would be mine."[13]

It was reported that the book sold nearly a half-million copies in its first few months, topping sales charts globally. Ken Tucker, writing in the *New York Times*, concluded after reading it, "In the end it seems that, like Elvis Presley, his only equal in pop-culture stature, Michael Jackson is a supremely

gifted and beloved artist who is held captive: by his upbringing, by his fame, by his power—by himself. For as much as his book reveals of his connection to the everyday world, he might as well be walking on the moon."[14] It made for a fascinating if only partially revealing read.

With all of the money that was coming his way, it was about time Jackson had himself a proper piece of real estate. Moving finally out of Hayvenhurst, Jackson bought 2,675 acres of land in 1988 in the Santa Ynez Valley in Santa Barbara County, California: 5225 Figueroa Mountain

Road, christened Neverland after the place where Peter Pan lived in Jackson's favorite book by J. M. Barrie. It became the greatest single manifestation of the scale of Jackson's success, a brick-and-mortar metaphor for Jackson himself: larger than life, with a lake, a zoo, its own railway line and stations, and, of course, the element that all the press would focus on, the funfair. It would be a controversial home for him.

As the *Bad* tour continued, fans had another memento of Jackson to keep in their hearts: *Moonwalker*, the ninety-two-minute *Bad* short-film compendium/concert film/autobiography. The film was originally intended to coincide with the release of the album; it eventually

came out in October 1988 in Europe, and was issued on videocassette in the United States in January 1989. It featured the soon-to-be Grammy Award–winning video for "Leave Me Alone," which had been issued as a bonus track on the *Bad* CD, and was released as a standalone single to coincide with the premiere of the film. The clip, directed by Jim Blashfield, is an amusing send up of Jackson's life, with an animated Jackson traveling in a carnival-ride capsule through the recent events of his life, with sensationalist newspaper headlines about Elephant Man bones and shrines to Elizabeth Taylor. The Colin Chilvers–directed "Smooth Criminal" sequence features Joe Pesci and some

immaculate dancing. Overall, *Moonwalker* was an indulgent and plotless vehicle for Jackson, but as a snapshot of the era, it remains an essential curio within the Jackson legend.

2300 JACKSON STREET

In 1989, the Jacksons—now Tito, Jackie, Jermaine, and Randy—returned for a final album; Michael was asked to participate but declined. As a result, while he guested on backing vocals on the title track of *2300 Jackson Street*, that was it. Released in May 1989, the album demonstrated that although the appetite for their brother was enormous, without him, they sadly were not the proposition they once were, Jermaine or no Jermaine. The following year, much to Joe Jackson's chagrin, Epic Records dropped the Jacksons.

On April 13, 1989, just ahead of that album's release, Elizabeth Taylor presented Jackson with the Heritage Award for Career Achievement and the Sammy Davis Jr. Award for Entertainer of the Year at the third Annual *Soul Train* Awards, proclaiming him, "in my estimation, the true king of pop, rock, and soul."

It had been a whirlwind time for Jackson; the '80s had very much been his decade. No single figure in popular music defined the era in the way he had. Although he had released only two albums, one was the biggest-selling of all time; the other one was the first to spawn five US No. 1 singles. With all his quirks and eccentricity, Michael Jackson had completely reinvented himself for a second decade of success.

The Jackson brothers promote 2300 Jackson Street, *1989.*

One of the principal reasons Bad *took so long to arrive was that the years 1983 to 1986 were such an incredibly complex rollercoaster ride of enormous success for Michael Jackson. There had been manias and crazes in popular music previously, but, spurred on by the globalization of media, there had simply been nothing like this. As singles continued to fall off* Thriller *like overripe apples from an over-verdant bough, Jackson was in enormous demand the world over.*

CHAPTER 8

YOU GOT ME SUPERSONIC, BABY

JACKSONMANIA

"Your deep faith in God and your adherence to traditional values are an inspiration to all of us."
—RONALD REAGAN, 1984

I'M NOT LIKE OTHER GUYS: MICHAEL JACKSON'S THRILLER

By late 1983, *Thriller* had a further extension to its already audacious lifecycle with the premiere of the fourteen-minute John Landis–directed film for the album's title track. It took the album from extremely successful pop record to little short of being a cultural icon. Casting the clean-cut, scandal-free singer as a werewolf in a short film was a risk, but one that truly paid off. Jackson had greatly admired the 1981 film *An American Werewolf in London*, so he engaged its director Landis on the project. Not only Landis was involved, however, as Jackson assembled a crew of some of the greatest talents working in horror films, including revered makeup artist Rick Baker, who had worked on *American Werewolf*, *The Howling*, and *Star Wars*.

Beginning with a disclaimer from Jackson—"Due to my strong personal convictions, I wish to stress that this film in no way endorses a belief in the occult"—*Michael Jackson's Thriller* opens with a scene in which he turns into a werecat and attacks his girlfriend (former *Playboy* centerfold Ola Ray). It transpires that we have been watching a movie, and, in fright, Jackson's girlfriend (Ray again) leaves the old-school picture house in which she and Jackson have been watching the film. As they walk home, Jackson begins to sing the song's verses to Ray; members of the undead from a nearby cemetery begin to rise from their graves as Vincent Price's narration begins. Within minutes,

OPPOSITE: *Michael Jackson waving to fans outside Madame Tussauds, London, March 1985.*

ABOVE: *One of the most famous images of the 1980s, if not the twentieth century: Jackson amid the zombies in* Thriller.
OPPOSITE: *The biggest-selling videocasette of its era:* Making Michael Jackson's Thriller.

the couple is surrounded by the undead; now begins the legendary sequence, choreographed by Jackson and Michael Peters, of Jackson zombifying and joining in a spectacular dance routine with the others. The impact of this scene can never be overestimated—and nor can how chilling it is. The zombies circle on Ray, and it looks as if Jackson is about to attack her. We realize she has simply fallen asleep on his sofa. It was all a dream. But as Jackson offers to take her home, his eyes flash zombie yellow.

The result was a truly groundbreaking piece of entertainment that merged music and film. It is an act of supreme confidence, of an artist completely at the peak of his game. Supposed to be a promotional video, it is not until four minutes into the film that we actually get to hear the record; the chorus itself won't appear until nine-and-a-half minutes in. From this point on, promotional videos for records became extravaganzas, and not merely pop stars singing their latest hits.

The video was shown on MTV in early December 1983, sending album sales stratospheric. Jackson's lawyer, John Branca, suggested that, as Jackson was funding this promo himself, a documentary should be made to coincide with it. MTV and the Showtime cable network financed the documentary, entitled *Making Michael Jackson's Thriller*, which was put on a sell-through videocassette alongside the promo. Released in the United States on December 14, it sold over five hundred thousand copies in its first month. By the time it was released in the UK at the end of March 1984, it was on its way to becoming the biggest-selling videocassette in the world at that point, ultimately selling in the region of nine million copies. It was said that the film added another fourteen million additional album and tape sales over the next six-month period.

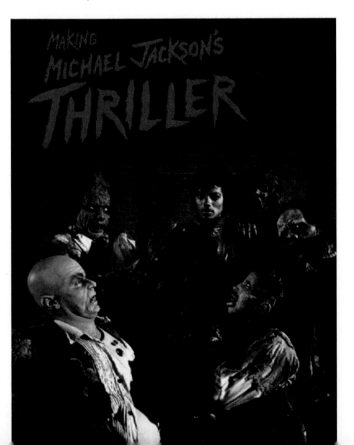

THE PEPSI INCIDENT

The year 1984 was a strange one for Michael Jackson. Although commercially it can be seen as the very apex of his career, it could be argued that the events of January 27, 1984, were the pivotal moment in his life.

The Jacksons had signed a sponsorship deal with Pepsi and were filming a commercial at the Shrine Auditorium, Los Angeles, in front of an invited audience of 3,000, to simulate a concert. Michael, who was not a fan of Pepsi, didn't want to do it. During the sixth take of the commercial, which was to feature the brothers singing a song called "You're a Whole New Generation," a magnesium flash bomb went off too early, and Jackson's hair was caught aflame.

Jackson ran from stage, spinning around as if to dance away the fire, before the amassed crew put it out. As his head rose, the back of it clearly displayed a badly burned bald patch. Jackson was in agony. He was rushed to the Cedars-Sinai Medical Center before moving to the burn unit at Brotman Medical Center in Culver City. Ever the showman, he asked for his single diamante-studded glove so that he could raise a hand to the cameras as he was stretchered in.

Jackson had third-degree burns. He was in acute pain and, as he had always done, he refused painkillers. However, the smarting was so great that he gave in and took the Darvocet and Percocet.[1] This was to be the beginning of his dependency. It could be argued that these were the remnants of his youth going up in a smoldering pyre.

Pepsi settled out of court, with Jackson donating the $1.5 million award to the Brotman Medical Center. The whole of America held its breath for his recovery. In February, Thomas

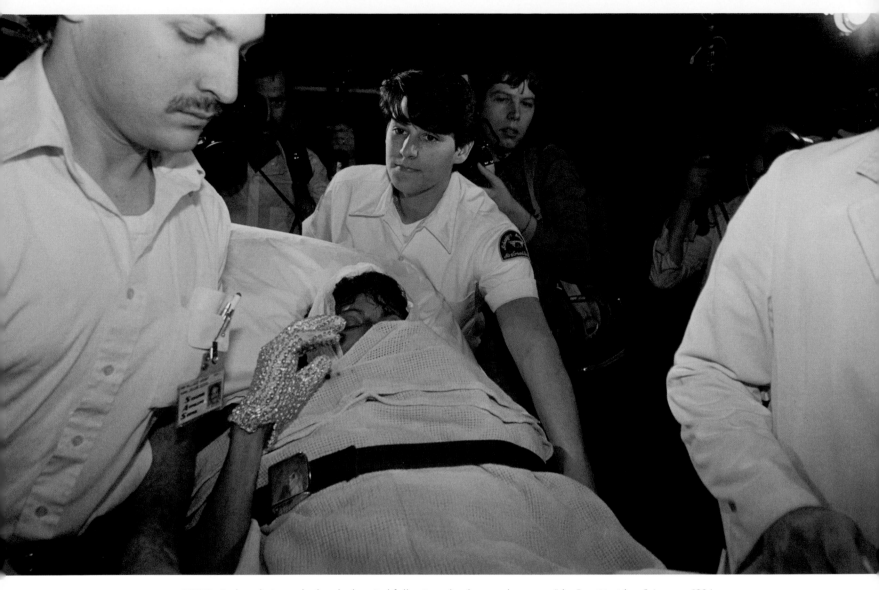

ABOVE: *Jackson being rushed to the hospital following what became known as "the Pepsi incident," January 1984.*
OPPOSITE: *CBS Records president and CEO Walter Yetnikoff.*

Wyman, the president and chairman of CBS, read out a telegram on national television from "an out-of-town fan." It read, "Dear Michael, I was pleased to learn that you are not seriously hurt in your recent accident. All over America, millions of people look up to you as an example. Your deep faith in God and your adherence to traditional values are an inspiration to all of us. Especially young people searching for something real to believe in. You've gained quite a lot of fans along the road since 'I Want You Back' and Nancy and I are among them. Keep up the good work, Michael, we are happy for you. Sincerely, Ronald Reagan." In May of that year, Jackson would visit the White House and receive a special award from the president for his work with charities that helped people overcome alcohol and narcotic abuse.

THE THRILLER JUGGERNAUT AND THE GRAMMY AWARDS

In the week following Jackson's accident, *Thriller* reportedly gained seven hundred thousand extra sales. Soon enough, it had become a greatest-hits package—seven of its nine tracks were issued as singles, and the *Thriller* video kept its profile sky high. As Walter Yetnikoff recalled, "Michael's passion for world conquest was singular. I knew all about burning ambition—my own and those of other execs and artists. But Michael's drive bordered on the psychopathic. He lived, breathed, slept, dreamt, and spoke of nothing but No. 1 successes."[2] Jackson would phone for his daily sales figures and chide Yetnikoff if *Thriller* slipped from the top spot in the United States.

The *Guinness Book of World Records* announced that *Thriller*, having shifted twenty-five million units, was the biggest-selling album ever. Jackson was presented with a special edition of the book by its co-founder, Norris McWhirter, at an event held at the Museum of Natural History in New York, on February 7, less than two weeks after the burning incident.

These breathtaking statistics were paraded to an audience of the great and the good—sixty-seven Gold Awards and fifty-eight Platinum Awards in twenty-eight countries on six continents. With his strange blend of hauteur and crippling self-doubt, Jackson told the crowd that "for the first time in my life, I feel like I've accomplished [something] as I'm in the *Guinness Book of World Records*." It was one of the most popular books with children, and something Jackson had been fascinated with for years. Although it was ironically the *Motown 25* TV special that had broken Jackson again, he very

pointedly stated that CBS was "the best record company in the world" in his speech, calling Yetnikoff the "best record company president in the world."

The 26th Annual Grammy Awards were held that year on February 28 at the Shrine Auditorium in Los Angeles. Jackson returned one month and one day after his hair had caught fire at the same venue. *Thriller* moonwalked away with no less than eight Grammys—a record at the time. After *Off the Wall's* disappointing showing three years earlier, Jackson was vindicated.

A STATE OF SHOCK: VICTORY

One of the strangest missteps at this point in Jackson's career was his decision to return to his brothers when he could have gone out and

ABOVE: *Jackson with Quincy Jones at the 1984 Grammy Awards.* OPPOSITE: *The* Victory *tour announcement with Don King, 1983.*

commanded the world's stages alone. However, the *Victory* album and tour provided the opportunity to unite all six brothers for the first time, now that Jermaine had returned to the fold after the *Motown 25* special. It was mainly a case of financial expediency for the brothers. In November 1983, Jackson informed Walter Yetnikoff that the tour and album was happening, and although he was not happy about it and had originally fought against participating in it, it was something his mother wanted to happen. If Katherine wanted it, Michael could not refuse.

With the Jackson brothers represented by their father Joe and the flamboyant boxing promoter Don King, Michael wanted a bulwark against this and enlisted the services of Frank

DiLeo, the larger-than-life vice president of national promotion at Columbia to manage him, in conjunction with John Branca. After all, if DiLeo had been largely responsible for the marketing phenomenon of Thriller, there must surely be plenty he could do for Jackson himself.

The next five years would be the most supersonic of Michael Jackson's career, but *Victory* was arguably the least consequential long-player the Jackson brothers put out. The weight of expectation was enormous; people were waiting for something truly wondrous. Instead, it was an extremely workmanlike album

for which the brothers were rarely in the studio at the same time.

Michael has two significant solo tracks on the album. The first is "State of Shock," a grinding rock duet with Mick Jagger that he originally intended to sing with Queen front man Freddie Mercury. It was released as the album's lead single, reaching No. 3 in the United States but only No. 14 in the UK. It was good, but not good enough.

His co-write with Marlon, "Be Not Always," finds him employing the close-miked pathos of "She's Out of My Life," offering tender relief from the grind of the rest of the album. Otherwise, his

MICHAEL JACKSON | TIMELINE

1950s–1960s

1958 | August 29: Michael Jackson is born in Gary, Indiana.

1962 | Michael Jackson performs "Climb Every Mountain" for his kindergarten class; Tito, Jackie, and Jermaine form their first vocal group.

1963 | Marlon and Michael join their brothers in the group and play their first professional show.

1964 | The group plays talent shows in the Gary area.

1965 | The Jackson brothers win a talent contest at Roosevelt High School, singing the Temptations' "My Girl."

1966 | The Jackson Brothers make their debut at Gary nightclub Mister Lucky's Lounge.

1967 | August: After the Jackson Brothers support her in concert, Gladys Knight brings the group to Berry Gordy's attention.

1968 | January 30: "Big Boy"/"You've Changed" is released by Steeltown Records.
July 12: The Jackson Brothers support Bobby Taylor & the Vancouvers in concert, who then set up an audition for them at Motown.
July 23: The Jackson Brothers audition for Motown vice presidents Ralph Seltzer and Suzanne de Passe at Hitsville, Detroit. A 16mm film is made and sent to Berry Gordy in Los Angeles.
July 26: Ralph Seltzer offers Joseph Jackson a recording contract with Motown Records.
November 25: The Jackson Brothers play Berry Gordy's Christmas party.

1969 | January 31: The Jackson family relocates to Los Angeles.
August 11: Diana Ross presents the Jackson 5 to the public at The Daisy discotheque in Beverly Hills.
October 7: "I Want You Back" is released by Motown.
December 14: The Jackson 5 appear on *The Ed Sullivan Show*.
December 18: *Diana Ross Presents the Jackson 5* is released.

1970s

1970 | January 31: "I Want You Back" goes to the US No. 1 spot.
February 24: "ABC" is released.
May 8: *ABC* is released.
May 2: The Jackson 5 make their first headlining appearance at the Philadelphia Convention Center.
August 28: "I'll Be There" is released.
September 8: *Third Album* is released.
October 15: *Jackson 5 Christmas Album* is released.
October 16: The Jackson 5 headline Madison Square Garden, New York City.

1971 | January 31: The Jackson 5 return home to Gary for two benefit concerts for mayor Richard Hatcher. They are given the key to the city and the concerts are filmed.
March 16: "Never Can Say Goodbye" is released.
April 12: *Maybe Tomorrow* is released.
April 18: The Jackson 5 appear on Diana Ross' ABC TV special, *Diana!*
September 11: The *Jackson 5ive* cartoon series begins broadcasting on ABC.
September 19: The *Goin' Back to Indiana* TV special is broadcast on ABC.
September 29: *Goin' Back To Indiana* is released.

October 7: Michael Jackson's first solo single, "Got to Be There," is released by Motown.
December 27: *The Jackson 5 Greatest Hits* is released.

1972 | January 24: Michael Jackson's debut solo album, *Got to Be There*, is released.
May 23: *Looking Through the Windows* by the Jackson 5 is released.
July 22: "Ben," the theme to the film of the same name, by Michael Jackson is released.
August 4: *Ben*, Michael Jackson's second solo album, is released.
October 30: The Jackson 5 appear at the Royal Command Performance, London Palladium, England.
November 5: The *Royal Variety Performance* is broadcast on UK television.
November 8: At a taping of *Top of the Pops*, the Jackson 5 perform "Lookin' Though the Windows."

1973 | February: "Doctor My Eyes" is released by the Jackson 5 and becomes a UK Top 10 hit.
March 27: Michael Jackson sings "Ben" at the Academy Awards.
March 29: *Skywriter* by the Jackson 5 is released.
April 13: *Music & Me* by Michael Jackson is released.
July: The Jackson 5's world tour reaches Australia.
August 3: "Get It Together" by the Jackson 5 is released.
September 12: *G.I.T—Get It Together* by the Jackson 5 is released.
November 3: The Jackson 5 appear on *Soul Train*, performing "Dancing Machine." Michael Jackson demonstrates his robot dance.

1974 | February 19: "Dancing Machine" by the Jackson 5 is released.

April 9: The Jacksons' Las Vegas residency begins.
August 7: Stevie Wonder's "You Haven't Done Nothin'," featuring the Jackson 5 on backing vocals, is released.
September 5: *Dancing Machine* by the Jackson 5 is released.
November 7: "You Haven't Done Nothin' " tops the US charts.

1975 | January 16: *Forever, Michael* is released.
May 15: *Moving Violation*, the final Jackson 5 album recorded for Motown, is released.
June 30: The Jacksons announce their departure from Motown to Columbia at a press conference. The deal brings better terms and improved creative control, but leads to wrangling with Motown over their departure.

1976 | February 13: The Jackson 5 play their final formal engagements on a six-date engagement in Manila, the Philippines.
June 16: *The Jacksons* TV series begins broadcasting on CBS.
October 26: *Joyful Jukebox Music*, the first of Motown's compilations with unreleased music by the Jackson 5, is released.
October 29: "Enjoy Yourself," the first single by the Jacksons, is released.
November 27: *The Jacksons* is released on Epic Records.

1977 | March 14: "Dreamer" by the Jacksons is released.
May: The Jacksons appear as part of a Royal Command Performance to honor the Queen's Silver Jubilee in Glasgow.
June 25: "Show You the Way to Go" gives the Jacksons their first and only UK No. 1.
June 20: Michael Jackson attends Studio 54 in New York City for the first time.
Summer: Rehearsals and filming of *The Wiz* take place in New York City.
October 18: *Goin' Places* by the Jacksons is released.

1978 | October 26: *The Wiz* premieres and its soundtrack album and "Ease on Down the Road" is released.
December 17: *Destiny* by the Jacksons is released.
December 21: "You Can't Win," Michael Jackson's first solo single on Epic, is released.

1979 | January 16: *Boogie!*, another collection of Motown-era Jackson 5 outtakes, is released.
January 27: "Shake Your Body (Down to the Ground)" is released by the Jacksons.
July 28: "Don't Stop 'til You Get Enough" is released by Michael Jackson.
August 10: *Off the Wall* is released by Michael Jackson.
October: "Rock with You" is released as a single from *Off the Wall*.

1980s

February: "Off the Wall" is released.
March: "She's Out of My Life" is released.
April: Michael Jackson becomes the first solo artist to have four US Top 10 singles from the same album.
September 26: *Triumph* by the Jacksons is released.

1981 | March 25: "One Day in Your Life" and the album of the same name are released. The single becomes Michael Jackson's first UK No. 1.
July 8: The Jacksons' US *Triumph* tour begins in Memphis.
November 11: *The Jacksons Live!* is released.

1982 | April 14: Recording sessions begin for *Thriller*.
June: Michael Jackson records a spoken-word version of the forthcoming *E.T.* soundtrack.
October: "The Girl Is Mine," Michael's duet with Paul McCartney, is released.
September: "Muscles" by Diana Ross, written and produced by Michael Jackson, is released.
November 8: The *Thriller* recording sessions conclude.
November 30: *Thriller* is released.

1983 | January 2: "Billie Jean" is released.
February 14: "Beat It" is released.
March 25: *Motown 25: Yesterday, Today, and Tomorrow* is recorded at the Pasadena Civic Auditorium.
May 8: "Wanna Be Startin' Somethin' " is released.
May 16: *Motown 25: Yesterday, Today, and Tomorrow* is broadcast on NBC.
Mid-October: The *Thriller* video is filmed.
July 8: "Human Nature" is released.
September 19: "P.Y.T. (Pretty Young Thing)" is released.
November 30: The Jacksons announce their *Victory* album and tour for the following year.
December 2: *Michael Jackson's Thriller* premieres in the US.
December 3: *Michael Jackson's Thriller* premieres in the UK.

1984 | January 23: "Thriller" is finally released as a single.
January 27: Michael Jackson's hair catches fire during the filming of a Pepsi commercial at the Shrine Auditorium, Los Angeles.
February 7: The *Thriller Guinness Book of World Records* event takes place at the Museum of Natural History, New York City.
February 28: *Thriller* wins a record eight Grammy Awards.
May 17: *Farewell, My Summer Love* by Michael Jackson is released.
June 5: "State of Shock" by the Jacksons is released, featuring Mick Jagger.

July 2: *Victory* by the Jacksons is released.
July 6: The *Victory* tour begins at Arrowhead Stadium, Kansas City.
July 20: A Michael Jackson doll, officially approved by the star, goes on sale for $13.
September 5: Michael Jackson issues a statement, read by manager Frank DiLeo, dispelling rumors surrounding his private life.
November 20: Michael Jackson receives a star on the Hollywood Walk of Fame.

1985 | January 28: "We Are the World" is recorded.
February 26: *Making Michael Jackson's Thriller* wins Best Video Album at the 27th Annual Grammy Awards.
March 7: "We Are the World" is released.
March 26: Jackson visits the UK; two days later, he unveils a waxwork of himself at Madame Tussauds and visits the bones of John Merrick at the Royal London Hospital, Whitechapel.
April 13: "We Are the World" becomes a US No. 1 single.
April 20: "We Are the World" becomes a UK No. 1 single
August 10: Michael Jackson buys the ATV Catalogue, which means he now owns the copyright for the majority of the Beatles' publishing.

1986 | February 25: Michael Jackson and Quincy Jones attend the 28th Grammy Awards ceremony, picking up four awards for "We Are the World."
July 30: Michael attends the funeral of Vincent Minnelli, the father of his friend Liza Minnelli.
September 12: *Captain EO* is unveiled at Epcot Future World.

OPPOSITE: *Jackson with Frank DiLeo at Heathrow Airport, 1985.* ABOVE AND LEFT: *Michael takes center stage during the Victory tour.*

September 16: A *National Enquirer* front cover depicts Jackson sleeping in an oxygen chamber.

1987 | January 5: Recording sessions begin for Michael Jackson's *Bad*.
July 9: *Bad* recording sessions end.
July 13: CBS executives hear a playback of *Bad* at Jackson's Encino home.
July 20: "I Just Can't Stop Loving You" is released.
August 31: *Bad* is released.
September 7: "Bad" is released.
September 12: The *Bad* tour begins in Japan.
November 9: "The Way You Make Me Feel" is released.

1988 | January 16: "Man in the Mirror" is released.
February 1: *Moonwalk* is published.
April 18: "Dirty Diana" is released.
July 11: "Another Part of Me" is released.
July 16: Jackson plays Wembley Stadium with Princess Diana in attendance.
August: Jackson buys Neverland Ranch in Santa Barbara County, California.
October 21: "Smooth Criminal" is released.
October 29: The *Moonwalker* videocassette is released.

1989 | February: "Leave Me Alone" is released.
February 14: Michael Jackson parts company with manager Frank DiLeo.
April 13: Elizabeth Taylor presents Jackson with the Heritage Award for Career Achievement and the Sammy Davis Jr. Award for Entertainer of the Year at the third annual *Soul Train* Awards, proclaiming him, "in my estimation, the true king of pop, rock, and soul."
March 16: "2300 Jackson Avenue" by the Jacksons is released.
May 28: *2300 Jackson Avenue* by the Jacksons is released.
July 4: "Liberian Girl" is released in Europe and Australia.

1990s

1990 | April 5: Michael Jackson is honored as Entertainer of the Decade by President Bush in Washington, DC.
June: Recording sessions begin for what will become Michael Jackson's *Dangerous*.

1991 | March 25: Michael Jackson and Madonna arrive and sit together at the Academy Awards.
October 29: Recording sessions for *Dangerous* conclude.
November 11: "Black or White" is released.
November 14: The "Black or White" video premieres.
November 23: "Black or White" becomes Michael Jackson's first UK No. 1 since "I Just Can't Stop Loving You" in August 1987.
November 26: *Dangerous* is released.
December 7: "Black or White" reaches No. 1 in the US.

1992 | September 29: *The Jacksons: An American Dream*, the soundtrack to the TV documentary of the same name, is released.
November 23: "Heal the World" is released.

1993 | January 31: Michael Jackson performs "Jam," "Billie Jean," "Black or White," "We Are the World," and "Heal the World" at the Super Bowl XXVII halftime show.
February 10: Jackson appears on *The Oprah Winfrey Show*. The interview is watched by ninety million Americans.
May 1: Michael Jackson attends the World Music Awards with the Chandler family.
August 2: Jordan Chandler tells his father of alleged sexual relations with Michael Jackson.
August 4: Michael Jackson and Jordan Chandler

meet for the last time; Evan Chandler outlines his intentions to sue Jackson.
August 24: It is announced that Jackson is under investigation by the Los Angeles Police Department following allegations of child molestation against Jordan Chandler.
December 22: Jackson gives a televised speech from Neverland Ranch about the allegations.

1994 | January 25: Michael Jackson agrees to pay $22 million to Jordan Chandler and his parents, Evan and June Chandler.
May 26: Jackson marries Lisa Marie Presley.

1995 | May 31: "Scream" is released.
June 15: Jackson and Lisa Marie Presley appear with Diane Sawyer on ABC's *Primetime Live*.
June 20: *HIStory: Past, Present, and Future, Book 1* is released.
August 15: "You Are Not Alone" is released.
September 2: "You Are Not Alone" becomes the first single to ever debut at No. 1 on the *Billboard* Hot 100.
November 27: "Earth Song" is released.

1996 | January 18: Michael Jackson and Lisa Marie Presley separate.
February 19: Jackson wins Artist of a Generation and performs "Earth Song" at the BRIT Awards. Pulp front man Jarvis Cocker storms the stage and waves his behind at the audience.
August 20: Michael Jackson and Lisa Marie Presley divorce.
September: The first leg of the *HIStory* tour commences in Prague.
November 14: Jackson marries Debbie Rowe in a ceremony in Sydney, Australia.

1997 | January 1: Jackson signs a preliminary letter of intent to build a theme park in the Polish capital of Warsaw, joining hands with mayor Marcin Swiecicki.
February 13: Michael Joseph Jackson is born. He will be known as Prince.
May 19: *Michael Jackson's Ghosts* is released.
May 30: *Blood on the Dance Floor: HIStory in the Mix* is released.
May 31: The second leg of the *HIStory* tour commences in Bremen, Germany.

1998 | April 3: Paris-Michael Katherine Jackson is born.
July 19: Jackson attends Nelson Mandela's eightieth birthday party.

1999 | April 10: Jackson attends a Fulham FC match in London.
June 25: The first *Michael Jackson and Friends* concert takes place in Seoul, South Korea.
June 27: At *Michael Jackson and Friends* in Munich, the central section of a bridge Jackson walks across collapses, sending him plummeting to the ground.
October 8: Jackson divorces Debbie Rowe.

2000s

2000 | January 20: VH1 viewers vote "Billie Jean" the No. 1 song of the 1980s.

2001 | March 2: Michael Jackson is inducted into the Rock and Roll Hall of Fame.
September 7 and 10: *Michael Jackson: 30th Anniversary Special* takes place at Madison Square Garden, New York City.
August 22: "You Rock My World" is released.
September 13: The "You Rock My World" video premieres.
October 21: The *United We Stand* concert takes place.
October 30: *Invincible* is released.
December 3: "Cry" is released.

2002 | February 21: Prince Michael "Blanket" Jackson II is born in La Mesa, California.
June 14: Jackson attends an Exeter City FC football match with David Blaine and Uri Geller.
July 7: Jackson signs a will granting his mother custody of his three children if he dies while they are still minors.
November 19: Michael Jackson dangles his son Blanket over a hotel balcony in Germany.

2003 | February 3: *Living with Michael Jackson* airs in the UK on ITV.
February 6: *Living with Michael Jackson* airs in the US on ABC.
February 20: *Michael Jackson: The Footage You Were Never Meant to See* airs in the US on Fox.
February 24: *Michael Jackson: The Footage You Were Never Meant to See* airs in the UK on Sky One.
September 13: Neverland opens to the public for a once-in-a-lifetime event: a concert featuring Ashanti, with all the rides open.
November 17: *Michael Jackson Number Ones* is released in the UK.
November 20: "One More Chance," which is to become Michael Jackson's final single in his lifetime, is released.
November 20: Michael Jackson turns himself in to police investigating claims of abuse against Gavin Arvizo.

2004 | January 16: Jackson pleads not guilty to child molestation charges.
April 21: A grand jury indicts Jackson.
December 3: Law enforcement officers spend two days searching Neverland.

2005 | January 31: Case No. 133603: The People of the State of California v. Michael Joseph Jackson begins with the jury being selected.
June 13: Michael Jackson is acquitted of all charges.
October 10: Jackson causes pandemonium at Madame Tussauds in London when he appears with a new waxwork of him.

October 21: It is announced that Jackson has made Bahrain his new home.

2006 | April 18: Two Seas Records, a joint venture between Jackson and Abdulla bin Hamad Al-Khalifa, is announced.

2007 | March 10: Michael Jackson meets troops at US military base Camp Zama in Japan.

2008 | January 14: "The Girl Is Mine 2008," a duet with will.i.am, is released.
February 11: *Thriller 25* is released.
August 25: The *King of Pop* compilation is released.

2009 | January 7: Jackson leases a mansion in Holmby Hills, Los Angeles.
March 5: Jackson announces the *This Is It* concerts at the O2 Arena in London.
March 8: The longest-ever UK TV commercial airs for the *This Is It* concerts on ITV.
March 13: Tickets go on sale; all shows sell out within several hours.
May: Rehearsal begins at the Staples Center, Los Angeles.
June 25: Michael Jackson dies in Los Angeles, California.
July 7: A public memorial service for Jackson takes place at the Staples Center, Los Angeles.
October 28: *Michael Jackson: This Is It* premieres.

2010 | February 8: An inquest rules that Michael Jackson died as a result of negligence and an over-administration of Propofol.
March 16: Jackson's estate agrees to the terms of a new record deal with Sony.

December 10: *Michael*, the first posthumous collection of previously unreleased recordings by Michael Jackson, is released.

2011 | September 27: The trial of Jackson's doctor, Conrad Murray, begins.
November 21: *Immortal*, the soundtrack to Jackson's Cirque du Soleil show, is released.

2013 | April: The Jackson family files a lawsuit against concert promoter AEG.
October: A court rules against the Jackson family, stating that AEG had no knowledge of Jackson's drug dependency.

2014 | May 9: Sony releases *Xscape*, the second album of previously unreleased material by Jackson.

2016 | January 24: Spike Lee's *Journey from Motown to Off the Wall* premieres at the Sundance Film Festival.
February 5: *Journey from Motown to Off the Wall* debuts on Showtime.
February 26: A new *Off the Wall* CD/DVD package containing *Journey from Motown to Off the Wall* is released.
February 27: Quincy Jones files a lawsuit against the Jackson estate, claiming unpaid royalties.
March 14: It is announced that Sony is to buy out Jackson's share of ATV publishing for a reported $750 million dollars.

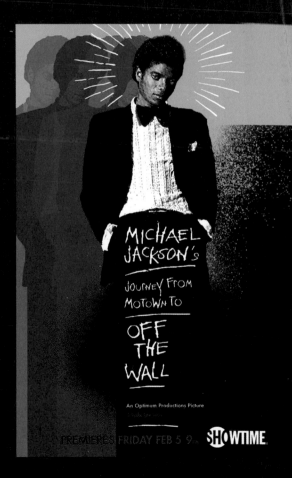

supporting vocals and co-writes can be found on tracks "The Hurt" and "Torture."

Victory was released on July 2, 1984; though only minimal publicity was undertaken for it, it was hardly a failure. It sold over seven million copies worldwide and reached No. 4 in the United States and No. 3 in the UK.

The tour to support the album was enormous, and, tellingly, the album it was nominally promoting was completely left out of the set list, save for a quick snatch of "State of Shock," which was incorporated into "Shake Your Body (Down to the Ground)." This was because Jackson simply refused to learn or rehearse tracks from it. The tour was dogged with controversy over high ticket prices; in a bid to outsmart resellers, prospective attendees could only purchase tickets by entering a lottery by mail in order to possibly "win" blocks of four tickets. Unsuccessful applicants would have their money refunded, but only after the profits had gone to the promoters. Jackson stepped in to quell the controversy,

LEFT: *The brothers in full regalia for the* Victory *tour.*
ABOVE: Victory *was released in a storm of publicity, yet it never quite clicked with the buying public.*

stating that he would be donating his share to charity, and normal ticket sales resumed.

Jackson was initially happy enough to be playing again with his brothers, with the collective approach taking away some of the pressure on him. But the tour, as spectacular as it was, did not brim over with the same bonhomie as the group's 1981 outing had done. As the tour progressed, Jackson could not help but wonder whether he should instead be out there promoting *Thriller* as a solo artist. Prince, who had been in the left field of African-American pop since the late '70s, had taken a leaf from Jackson's book and upped the white rock quotient of his work. As a result, his album and film *Purple Rain* seemed to pick up where *Thriller* left off, yet here was Jackson, promoting old records and a new album he didn't even like. He became distant from the brothers, even traveling separately from them.

Despite all these issues, the *Victory* tour was seen as a great success. The fifty-five dates grossed $75 million, which was a record at the time. Discussions were under way to continue the tour into Europe in 1985, but the show at Los Angeles' Dodger Stadium on December 9 was to be the final time in the twentieth century that the Jacksons appeared onstage together. There was considerable resentment in the Jackson camp when Michael pulled the plug on his brothers' future earning potential.

"WE ARE THE WORLD"

In 1984, Bob Geldof, the leader of the new-wave group the Boomtown Rats, phoned every pop star in England he knew (Duran Duran, Phil Collins, Boy George, etc.) and enlisted them to

hastily make a record called "Do They Know It's Christmas?" in response to the famine in Ethiopia. The single, released under the banner name Band Aid, raced to the top of the UK charts and became at that point the biggest-selling record of all time, with all the proceeds going to famine relief in Africa.

Lionel Richie's manager, Ken Kragen, was so inspired by what Bob Geldof had done that he felt compelled to start in motion an American equivalent. He had watched Geldof talk (*and he can talk*) on television about Band Aid with Harry Belafonte, who allegedly said that he was "ashamed and embarrassed at seeing a bunch of English kids doing what black Americans ought to have been doing."[3] Belafonte asked Quincy Jones if he would put together a record; Jones enlisted Jackson and Lionel Richie, and the two wrote a song almost straight away, with Jackson contributing most of the lyrics. It was called "We Are the World."

On January 28, 1985, more than forty-five of America's top musicians participated in the

recording. It was a remarkable scene—artists included Bob Dylan, Bruce Springsteen, Paul Simon, Stevie Wonder, Tina Turner, Billy Joel, Ray Charles, all in the same room. The only notable absentees were fellow summer 1958 birthdates Madonna and Prince. Bob Geldof was at the rehearsals and recording, and walked into the studios to find Jackson working with Jones alone; he was rehearsing vocals, and even at this early stage, it was sounding wonderful. As Jones asked for a fifth take, Geldof later wrote, "He did it again, in a voice of total purity. He was just practicing, but it could have been recorded as the finished product. It was a preposterous level of professionalism and talent."[4]

The collective name chosen for the ensemble was USA for Africa, and the single became a worldwide hit. "We Are the World" sold eight

OPPOSITE: "We Are the World," released in March 1985, topped the charts in seventeen countries. TOP: Michael Jackson with Stevie Wonder and Lionel Richie at the 1986 Grammy Awards. ABOVE: A marked-up music and lyric sheet from the "We Are the World" recording session.

million copies in the United States alone and raised countless dollars for Africa. The sentiment spilled over into the enormous UK/US concert Live Aid on July 13, 1985. Michael Jackson did not participate, however, citing work on his forthcoming film *Captain EO*.

IT'S ONLY A NORTHERN SONG

As inordinate amounts of money began to tumble through the door, Jackson decided that he had to acquire possessions beyond the material wealth he was accruing. While recording "Say, Say, Say" with Jackson in England, Paul McCartney, who owned many copyrights, including Buddy Holly's catalogue, alerted him to the powerful potential revenue stream generated by owning music-publishing rights. Jackson was impressed, and allegedly jested that one day he would buy the Beatles' catalogue. As a result, Jackson asked Branca to start buying catalogues on his behalf; his first two purchases were the early Dion hits "The Wanderer" and "Runaround Sue," as penned by songwriter Ernie Maresca. Further acquisitions followed, including the copyrights of the Sly and the Family Stone catalogue that had been so influential to the young Jackson.

In 1984, it became clear that the ATV Catalogue was coming up for sale. Founded by British impresario Lew Grade in 1955, it contained, among many precious copyrights, every song (bar a handful of early numbers) that John Lennon and Paul McCartney had written for the Beatles, and some early George Harrison songs as well. It was like

a holy grail to Jackson: the foundation that modern popular music stood upon could be his. The Beatles' work had been folded into ATV in 1969 when Grade bought Northern Songs, the company that was set up by Dick James and Brian Epstein to administer Lennon and McCartney's Beatles publishing. Lew Grade divested the company in 1982 to Australian businessman Robert Holmes à Court, who stripped it of many of its loss-making assets before putting it up for sale again. McCartney had engaged Lennon's widow, Yoko Ono, to see if she would be interested in purchasing the catalogue in the early '80s, and McCartney was offered first refusal this time around as well. Ultimately, however, the $47.5 million price tag was deemed too high.

After months of negotiations, John Branca purchased the catalogue on Michael Jackson's behalf on August 10, 1985. When McCartney was told, he said, "I think it's dodgy to do things like that. To be someone's friend and then to buy the rug they're standing on." Jackson tried to phone McCartney to reason with him, but the Beatle would not speak to him. "Paul's got a real problem," Jackson later said, "and I'm finished trying to be the nice guy. Too bad for him. I got the songs and that's the end of it."[5]

Although the two remained outwardly cordial for years, McCartney was deeply hurt. The purchase turned out to be arguably the shrewdest thing that Jackson ever did. The songs were certainly to keep Jackson afloat through his troubled later years.

Paul McCartney and Jackson clown for the cameras, December 1989.

Michael Jackson had a complex relationship with superstardom. He had known huge fame since he was eleven, but as we have seen, that was nothing compared with what was waiting just around the corner for him. He courted fame, he thought on a global scale, but as a shy individual, he abhorred the permanent lack of personal freedom and the machinations of the media. Few would have predicted the sheer scale and prolonged success of the album that Michael Jackson released on November 30, 1982. It was called Thriller.

CHAPTER 9

NO MERE MORTAL CAN RESIST

THRILLER AND MOTOWN 25

"Michael had once again reinvented himself, only this time as the third prong of pop's Holy Trinity—now it was Elvis, the Beatles, and Michael Jackson."

—WALTER YETNIKOFF[1]

Perhaps only Michael Jackson himself could have predicted the scale of success that *Thriller* was to experience. Having finished his touring commitments with his brothers, he was ready to record the follow-up to *Off the Wall*. This was to be no mere sequel: it would, quite simply, redefine popular music for the remaining years of the twentieth century and beyond.

There was one piece of business running concurrently with Jackson's plans: Steven Spielberg had asked if he would be interested in contributing a narration to the storybook soundtrack album accompanying his forthcoming film *E.T. the Extra-Terrestrial*. Jackson fell in love with the story and agreed, adding vocals as well to the album's love theme, "Someone in the Dark." Produced by the team Jackson was working with on *Thriller*, the narration was written by Spielberg, Quincy Jones, Jones' wife Peggy Lipton, and children's writer William Kotzwinkle. Jackson identified strongly with the alien with superpowers and broke down in tears on learning that he died in the story. He was to appear with the animatronic character on the cover of *Ebony* magazine around the film's release in November. He identified so much with the character that he kissed the plastic doll farewell when he finished the photo shoot, and gave him a "special thanks" credit on *Thriller*.

OPPOSITE: *Steve Barron's video for "Billie Jean" made Jackson a superstar the world over.*

STARLIGHT EXPRESS

Aside from recording the track "Muscles" for his friend Diana Ross, *E.T.* was the only significant distraction for Jackson that year; his time was now about ensuring that his next album would not only be *his* best ever, but one of *the* best ever. Recording of *Thriller* began in Studio A at Westlake Studios on Beverly Boulevard, Los Angeles, with "The Girl Is Mine" on Wednesday, April 14, and continued through to Monday, November 8, 1982. The album was mastered at Bernie Grundman's on the Thursday of that week, and was ready for sale on Tuesday, November 30, 1982.

In his final press interview before he died, Jackson outlined what he aimed for with the album: "Ever since I was a little boy, I would study composition. And it was Tchaikovsky that influenced me the most. If you take an album like *Nutcracker Suite*, every song is a killer, every one. So I said to myself . . . 'Why can't every song be so great that people would want to buy it if you could release it as a single?' So I always tried to strive for that. That was my purpose for the next album . . . I wanted to just put any one out that we wanted. I worked hard for it."[2]

He truly did work hard for it; the album was like an intricate jigsaw puzzle put together by the finest craftsmen. It was future pop, a mixture of light and shade that took the template of *Off the Wall* and completely reimagined it.

In reality, *Thriller* is the ultimate piece of showmanship. It's not all brilliant; in fact it could be argued that, overall, *Off the Wall* is better. *Thriller* is fundamentally five pleasant, above-average songs ("Baby Be Mine," "The Girl Is Mine," "P.Y.T.," "Human Nature," "The Lady in My Life") and then four of the most astonishing pop songs ever committed to tape ("Wanna Be Startin' Somethin'," "Thriller," "Beat It," and "Billie Jean").

In fact, the first recording was one of the most old-school numbers on the album: a Beatle and a Jackson meeting together, delivering some premium light entertainment. Jackson later said that "The Girl Is Mine" was one of his favorite songs to record, "because working with Paul McCartney was pretty exciting, and we just literally had fun. It was like lots of kibitzing and playing, and throwing stuff at each other, and making jokes. We actually recorded the track and the vocals pretty much live at the same time."[3]

LEFT: *Jackson singing with Diana Ross on her* Diana! *TV special, March 2, 1981.* OPPOSITE: *The smile says it all: Jackson entering Westlake Studios in Los Angeles, during the recording of* Thriller, *1982.*

Jackson was completely ready to work intensely to deliver a work of the highest standard. "The main part of *Thriller* only took three months to record," engineer Bruce Swedien told me in 2009. "That's the result of their musical understanding—talk about prepared, holy cow. Everything was written before it came to the studio. Most people would have been delighted to have material the strength of Michael's demos!"[4]

It was an album on which the detail simply ran riot: detail such as the four-foot-by-three-foot piece of Masonite-covered plywood trod heavily upon by Jackson, Steven Ray, and Nelson Hayes, known as the "bathroom stomp board" on the album's opener, "Wanna Be Startin' Somethin'." The phrase "everything but the kitchen sink" is often used to describe excess; here was everything including the "bathroom stomp board." It's three seconds of majesty, used once, that defines the whole album.

"The bathroom stomp board was Michael's idea," Swedien said. "We brought it in the studio, we had to mic it up, and he played it. Michael had drum cases set up that he would use as musical instruments . . . he always played those things himself."[5] Such was the album's detail.

If "The Girl Is Mine" is the album's broad invite for whites to join the party, "Wanna Be Startin' Somethin' " is one of Jackson's very best grooves, an overture equivalent to "Don't Stop 'til You Get Enough," locating Jackson at the leading edge of African-American pop. Its open referencing of Manu Dibango's "Soul Makossa," seen as the first ever disco record, was very clever; the polyrhythmic groove is still in the "Shake Your Body (Down to the Ground)" mode, but Jackson's skittering percussive vocal introduces another dimension, elevating the track from being merely another dance record.

Although two of his three compositions for the album were beautifully soulful ("Baby Be Mine" and the sweet "The Lady in My Life"), Rod Temperton came truly into his own on what was to become the album's title tack. "Rod was like Beethoven," Bruce Swedien told me. "When Rod brought a demo of a piece of music to the studio, every detail was complete. There was an incredible depth of music with Rod Temperton."

This was true of the demo called "Starlight" that Temperton had been toying with. "Starlight" would become "Thriller," one of the songs that would elevate the album to phenomenon status. Amazingly, it would become the album's *seventh* single when it was released in 1984, a full fifteen months after *Thriller*'s release. When Temperton wrote the song, an evocation of horror and the surreal, he had envisioned a narration at the end. He thought of a famous voice to deliver the performance. Peggy Lipton knew the actor Vincent Price and was happy to ask the question. Price was seventy-one years old at the time of recording, and although he had starred in a variety of films across the board, he had become, since the 1950s, synonymous with the horror genre, in

films such as *House of Wax*, *The Fly*, and, more recently, *The Abominable Dr. Phibes*. His sinister, velvety tones were instantly recognizable.

Price was no stranger to adding his voice to popular music; he had performed a monologue on Alice Cooper's 1975 album, *Welcome to My Nightmare*. The idea was that he would say some of his famous lines from his films. Jones felt, however, that Temperton should write something for him. Having agreed to do it ahead of the next day's 2 p.m. session, Temperton had clean forgotten he had an important meeting that he could not get out of, and ended up writing something on the spot. As a result, Temperton recalled, "it was one of those lucky times when it flowed out of me." He added a further couple of verses in the car on the way to Westlake. Price arrived at the same time, sat down, and read it through off pat; everything was captured in two takes. It was his bloodcurdling laugh at the end of the speech that gave the album its absolutely unique selling point.

It's hard to imagine now, but when *Thriller* was first released in late November 1982, there was almost a sense of misstep. "The Girl Is Mine" is good, but it was not a phenomenal choice as the lead single. Although it reached No. 2 on the US charts, it

OPPOSITE: *Bruce Swedien working his magic in the studio.*
ABOVE: *Jackson's handwritten lyrics to "Billie Jean."*
BELOW: *The European edition maxi-single of "Billie Jean."*

could have easily existed on an album from any point since Jackson started recording; it was like a Vegas number. The initial reviews were lukewarm. In the UK, Gavin Martin in *NME* was dismissive: "*Thriller* features the same team as its predecessor, though it uses nowhere near as many horns. This makes many of the tracks sound naked, especially when Quincy Jones' presence is barely felt. He coats everything with a sheen of glossy perfection rather than showering it with thunderbolts and manic invention."[6]

It was this glossy perfection, however, that caught on with audiences; this was the '80s, a time when surface was everything. When "Billie Jean" was released in January 1983, the album sprang into electrifying life. Originally titled "Not My Lover," it built on "Heartbreak Hotel" from *Triumph*. This slice of paranoia was Jackson at his zenith.

Alongside "Don't Stop 'til You Get Enough," "Billie Jean" is the most important record in the whole of Jackson's career. Sketched out as a demo initially by Jackson alone at home, it is amazing to see how the song arrived to the studio almost exactly as it ended. Quincy Jones was allegedly unsure about its inclusion, and certainly raised doubts over the length of the introduction. Considering the excess elsewhere on the album, though, the economy of the song is incredible, with Louis Johnson's watertight walking bass line and Ndugu Chancler's crisp snare to the fore. It is the end of the song that absolutely captivates: Jerry Hey's string arrangement, conducted by Jeremy Lubbock, played alongside David Williams' naggingly funky guitar. Bruce Swedien mixed the record multiple times before the second mix was allegedly chosen ahead of the others.

A story about an amalgam of groupies that followed the Jacksons on tour, it introduced one of pop's most notorious characters, leading to immediate speculation as to her identity. "There never was a real Billie Jean," Jackson writes in his autobiography. "This kind of thing has happened to some of my brothers and I used to be really amazed by it. I could never understand how these girls could say they were carrying someone's child when it wasn't true."[7] Elsewhere, it was stated that the song was based on an actual fan who claimed Jackson had fathered one of her twins; whoever it was based on, it became Jackson's calling card, and one of the principle reasons he remains idolized today.

The song's video did Jackson's bidding for him. The recently launched MTV had seen a wave of British acts explode on the US scene as acts from the UK mastered the art of the promo clip as a short film. As a result, Jackson contacted Steve Barron, one of the UK's hottest directors, to make a clip that was, despite the windy deserted street setting and photographer-in-pursuit backstory, in its way as simplistic as it sounds on the printed page: singer dances on under-lit pavement. But this was no ordinary singer; this was no ordinary dancer. Two and a half minutes in, there is a freeze-frame image that was to capture Jackson forever in the popular psyche. It became iconic. The video—packed full of early-'80s nonsense, oh, and a tiger—became the first video by an African-American artist to be put in heavy rotation. Helped by this, the record spent seven weeks at the top of the US charts; the showing of the video on MTV is reported to have added ten million additional sales to the album.

OPPOSITE: *On the set of the "Beat It" video, 1983.*

ABOVE: *Got to be there: the Jackson brothers reunite onstage for the first time since early 1976 at Motown 25.*
OPPOSITE: *Jackson's performance of "Billie Jean" at Motown 25 is one of the greatest moments in popular music of all time.*

With the record conquering the world's charts, Epic flipped out a follow-up, "Beat It," almost immediately. Jackson wrote the song as an exercise in making some rock music that he himself would enjoy; that sounded different to what was currently out there. With its strong anti-violence message, the record sounded unlike anything else that was around at the time. Jones called in Eddie Van Halen, who, after repeatedly thinking he was receiving a crank call, acquiesced and came down to the studio to perform what was to become his most heard solo of all time.

Commercials director Bob Giraldi helmed the video for "Beat It." It cast Jackson as a peacemaker halting the battle between two rival gangs as they square up for a showdown in a warehouse. After a balletic fight sequence, Jackson leads the gangs in highly choreographed dancing. Using real gangs gave the video a tremendous authenticity—and, most importantly, gave MTV another eagerly received video to put into heavy rotation. The single soared to No. 1 and gave its parent album an aura of invincibility.

MOTOWN 25

Michael Jackson's appearance at *Motown 25: Yesterday, Today, Forever* was simply revelatory. The brainchild of Suzanne de Passe, this TV special, recorded at the Civic Auditorium in Pasadena on March 25, 1983, was broadcast on NBC on May 16 of that year. It was a once-in-a-lifetime show designed to celebrate the label's twenty-fifth birthday. There were many highlights, with all of Motown's major hit-makers appearing onstage. This was a TV show for people who were not hip to the MTV sound,

reaching out far beyond that; in fact, it was Middle America writ large.

Jackson was finishing some edits on "Beat It" at Motown's studios in Los Angeles, when he encountered his old boss, Berry Gordy, who asked him to take part in the celebration. Gordy wanted him to reunite with his brothers, with Jermaine back in the fold. Jackson understandably wanted nothing to do with it. "I said no because of the *Thriller* thing," Jackson told *Ebony* magazine in 2007. "I was building and creating something." Gordy persevered, leading Jackson to give him an ultimatum. "I said, 'I will do it, but the only way I'll do it is if you let me do one song that's not a Motown song.' He said, 'What is it?' I said, ' "Billie Jean." ' He said, 'Okay, fine.' . . . So I rehearsed and choreographed and dressed my brothers, and picked the songs, and picked the medley. And not only that, you have to work out all the camera angles."[8]

Gordy was shrewd. Never one to miss an opportunity, he knew that Jackson's appearance would propel his spectacular to huge viewing figures and gain additional revenue through the sell-through video business. He would have the hottest artist in the known universe performing the biggest hit of the year. And what a performance it was.

In their spangled finery—with Michael sporting the single white glove that he had taken to wearing at the start of the '80s, having decided that wearing two "seemed so ordinary"—the original Jackson 5 reunite first for the two-song medley of "I Want You Back" and "The Love You Save," with Randy joining them at the end. Then, with all six onstage, the brothers run through "Never Can Say Goodbye" and an impassioned "I'll Be There." They are clearly enjoying the moment, and Michael seems genuinely touched to be back in his old role—and to see Jermaine, returned to stage left, behind his bass. When Jermaine sings his verse in "I'll Be There," Michael holds the microphone for him; they hold hands before embracing. Although a little awkward, it is a rather touching moment, and the emotion remains when all the brothers huddle closer for the final verse. All the training that Joe had put them through in that room in Gary still rings true.

Then, the brothers take their bow and depart from the stage, leaving Jackson alone. "I like those songs a lot," he says, "but especially . . . I like the new songs."

Ndugu Chancler's beat to "Billie Jean" kicks in, Jackson grabs a fedora (snuck out to him by assistant Nelson Hayes), and it is like the entire auditorium has been plugged in. And then, halfway through, he moonwalks—two two-second bursts of the movement that would cause an absolute sensation. Exactly who taught Jackson to moonwalk—or "glide," as it was known—is, like many Jackson landmarks, open to interpretation. It is commonly thought that Derek (Cooley) Jackson and Geron (Caszper) Canidate, who were dancers on *Soul Train*, taught Jackson the move, yet it had been popularized in the UK the year previously by Jeffrey Daniel, one-third of Shalamar, who had also been a dancer for years on *Soul Train* (on which Jackson had often appeared). A similar move had been used in films for years. Whatever—it didn't matter. The move was now Jackson's.

Journalists watched open-mouthed. As Charles Shaar Murray later wrote, "He sang the taut, tense masterpiece of sexual paranoia whilst unveiling state-of-the-art dance moves: some borrowed from young street dancers but all customized to his own spectacular skills. And then he did the 'moonwalk': moving forward whilst seeming to move backward. The audience in the hall erupted: seated at home in front of their TVs, so did the viewing public."[9] As Tom Graves was to write in *Rock & Roll Disc*, "Standing by himself in front of millions of viewers, including every peer he ever had at Motown, Michael Jackson electrified the audience down to its fingertips. It was a performance no less memorable than Elvis and the Beatles' *Ed Sullivan* appearances. Michael's stage moves were a *tour de force* and his vocals full-bodied, assured, and mature. To anyone watching it was obvious Michael Jackson was *the* star of the '80s."[10]

When Jackson came offstage, he was greeted by Marvin Gaye, the Temptations, Smokey Robinson, and his brothers, all hugging and kissing him. Richard Pryor informed him that it was the greatest performance that he had ever seen. "That was my reward," he told *Ebony* magazine twenty-five years later. "These were people who, when I was a little boy in Indiana, I used to listen to . . . Marvin Gaye, the Temptations, and to have them bestow that kind of appreciation on me, I was just honored. Then the next day, Fred Astaire called and said, 'I watched it last night, and I taped it, and I watched it again this morning. You're a helluva mover. You put the audience on their ASS last night!'"[11]

Jackson wasn't satisfied. He wanted more. His view was changed, he recalled, by a child he saw in the wings, who asked him, "Who taught you to move like that?"

"I guess God . . . and rehearsal," Jackson replied.[12]

The show provided another surge of sales for *Thriller*; and the singles just kept on coming. Around the time of the show's broadcast in May 1983, "Wanna Be Startin' Somethin' " was released, reaching the US Top 5; "Human Nature" followed in July, reaching No. 7; in September, "P.Y.T. (Pretty Young Thing)" hit No. 10, keeping the album high in the charts. The *Motown 25* performance put Jackson into the stratosphere.

Now, however, he felt he needed proper representation. In August 1983, Jackson asked Sony promotions man Frank DiLeo to become his manager. DiLeo was a big, brash businessman—he looked so much like a music industry manager he almost was a caricature. With DiLeo and the full might of CBS behind him, it was from here that

"Say Say Say" was undoubtedly the best collaboration between McCartney and Jackson.

the cult of Jackson began. As Walter Yetnikoff writes, "He literally resculpted his image, chose young children and chimps as companions, slept in oxygen chambers and consciously cultivated the crass mass media—including supermarket tabloids—to focus on his fame."[13]

With this image in place, *Thriller* reached its first birthday. "Love it or hate it, *Thriller* is pop's great, immovable Everest," the BBC was to report in 2009. "Marketing departments realized that more and more singles could be pulled from a record to prolong its shelf life, and Michael Jackson became the King of Pop with the whole of the recording industry at his investiture."[14]

"SAY SAY SAY"

While all of this mania was beginning to build, in September 1983, the final pieces of the Paul McCartney–Michael Jackson working-relationship jigsaw puzzle were put together, ready for their release on McCartney's *Pipes of Peace* album. The relationship had begun when Jackson phoned up McCartney on Christmas Day 1980 to suggest a collaboration, given that "Girlfriend" had been such a key song for Jackson on *Off the Wall*. Although it was recorded later, "The Girl Is Mine" had been such a pivotal number on *Thriller*.

The pair continued their collaboration on two more tracks; first was the beautiful, Isley Brothers–influenced album track "The Man," and the second was the worldwide chart smash "Say Say Say." The pair had begun recording "Say Say Say" in May 1981 in London, and it was completed at Cherokee Studios in Los Angeles in February 1983, with George Martin overseeing. A jaunty song that played to both artists' strengths, it benefitted from a video, again directed by Bob Giraldi. The "short film" broke new ground, as it followed hucksters "Mac" and "Jack" as they traveled America around (with McCartney's wife Linda) in a wagon, scamming Western frontier crowds by day and performing vaudeville shows by night. The video was notable for being the first to introduce dialogue into the narrative.

When the record hit No. 1 in the United States, it was a statistician's dream: the union of two of the three artists in the world who had sold over one hundred million records both as solo artists and as part of a group. Between them, at this point, they had had thirty-seven No. 1s. The relationship would not always be so rosy.

Adding finishing touches to "Say Say Say" in the studio, February 1983.

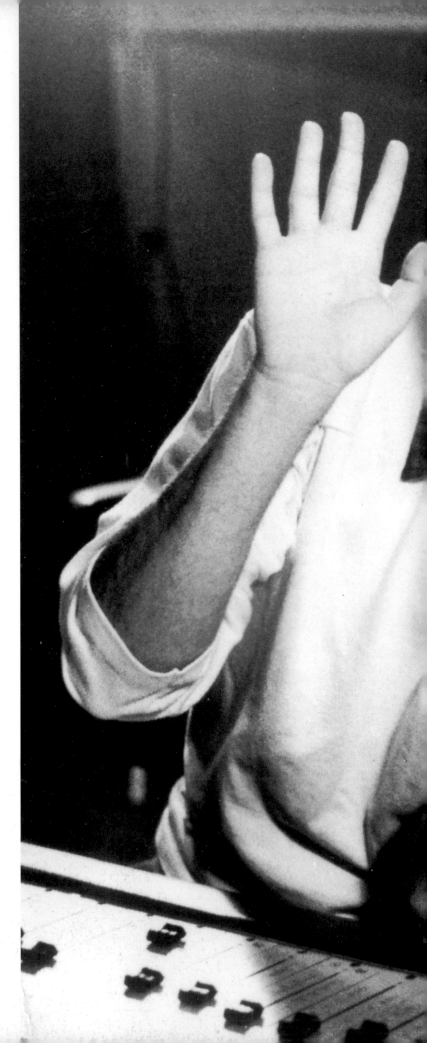

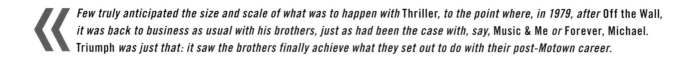

Few truly anticipated the size and scale of what was to happen with Thriller, *to the point where, in 1979, after* Off the Wall, *it was back to business as usual with his brothers, just as had been the case with, say,* Music & Me *or* Forever, Michael. Triumph *was just that: it saw the brothers finally achieve what they set out to do with their post-Motown career.*

CHAPTER 10

THE STARS DO SHINE

TRIUMPH

"Triumph gave us that final burst of energy we needed to put together a perfect show."

—MICHAEL JACKSON[1]

nstead of capitalizing on the success of *Off the Wall* with a solo tour, Jackson picked up again with his brothers, performing on the tour to promote *Destiny*, which had begun in January 1979 in Europe and continued intermittently throughout the year until ending in Nassau in December.

As 1980 dawned, *Off the Wall* continued to sell. "Rock with You" hit the US top spot in January and remained there for four weeks. The album maintained its high position in the world's charts throughout the year, buoyed by further singles being released until July of that year. This brought Jackson to a whole new level of success. Because of it, Motown began dipping into Jackson's back catalogue. Inspired by the success of "She's Out of My Life," Motown issued the *Forever, Michael* album track "One Day in Your Life" in May 1981. Although only a minor hit in the United States, it provided Jackson with his first ever solo UK No. 1 when it topped the charts for two weeks in June and July of that year. The appetite for Michael Jackson seemed insatiable.

TRIUMPH

Recorded across a year between June 1979 and June 1980, *Triumph* was an enormous record for the Jacksons, and the only one entirely composed by the brothers themselves. Released in late September 1980, it was a transitional album, catching Michael between *Off the Wall* and *Thriller*. If you add in *Destiny* as well, these represent the four records on which the entire Michael Jackson legacy rests.

OPPOSITE: *Michael Jackson leading his brothers on the* Destiny *tour at the Rainbow Theatre, London, 1979.*

OPPOSITE AND ABOVE: *The* Destiny *tour saw some of the best performances the Jacksons ever played.*

The nine self-produced tracks make for arguably the most consistent album the Jacksons released. It was to be their first to top the *Billboard* R&B charts since *Maybe Tomorrow* in 1971. The album was trailed by the dance-floor stomp of "Lovely One," which Jackson later summed up as an extension of "Shake Your Body (Down to the Ground)" with the added injection of the lighter sound of *Off the Wall*.[2] Released as a single in April 1980, it reached No. 12 on the *Billboard* Hot 100, laying the commercial foundations for *Triumph*.

At its zenith, the album equals Jackson's best material, whether with the brothers or solo. Although not the scale of hit Jackson may have liked, "Heartbreak Hotel" is as significant in his catalogue as "Don't Stop 'til You Get Enough" as it was his first major story song. Opening with a scream from sister LaToya, it uses the narrative in the way Jackson would for many of his later hits, most notably "Billie Jean." It is an ambitiously dark record centered on revenge, some miles away from burning out the dance floor. "I was trying to step into the future with ['Heartbreak Hotel'] trying something different, integrating drama and sound effects with music," Jackson later recalled, "and it worked."[3] Because of concerns about confusion with the Elvis Presley hit of the same name, the track was somewhat bewilderingly retitled "This Place Hotel."

It was down to the album's opening track to provide the album with its full commercial breakthrough: "Can You Feel It" captures the brothers having the most wonderful time, stretching out, with a nine-piece children's choir and a nineteen-piece adult choir (including Jim Gilstrap and Venetta Fields). It was Jackie Jackson who thought of incorporating the choirs in the mix, allowing the track to straddle the boundaries

of rock, soul, and gospel; Michael was to say, "That was a nod to Gamble and Huff, in a way, because the song was a celebration of love taking over, cleansing the sins of the world."[4] It certainly is a deeply powerful, moving song, preaching global unity. It was to become a fantastic set opener for the group, and a Top 10 single on both sides of the Atlantic. (It was also accompanied by an in-era space-age promotional film.) The other absolute standout is "Walk Right Now," built around Nathan Watts' hypnotic bass and Ollie Brown's metronomic drums. The seemingly endless, hypnotically repetitive groove leaves little doubt that the brothers had the potential to be the kings of the dance floor.

OPPOSITE: *Signing a record for pop-artist Andy Warhol, Madison Square Garden, New York City, August 19, 1981.*
ABOVE: *The Jacksons relaxing backstage at the Nassau Coliseum, New York, 1980.*

Triumph has aged the best of all the Jacksons' albums: as I was to write in a retrospective review for the BBC, "If you lived through it, you'll realize you're familiar with all of the tracks, as they seemed to be everywhere at the time—such as the swooning urban soundscape of 'Everybody' or the tender balladry of 'Time Waits for No One.' If you didn't hear it then, it's a sumptuous where-to-go-next after hearing the best of Michael's solo career."[5] The album simply did not disappoint; as *Blues and Soul* said on its release, it was "destined to become a major, major hit for the talented brothers—and deservedly so, because this album is the perfect continuation to Destiny."

LIVE!

The release of *Triumph* was preceded by four dates at the Forum in Los Angeles in September 1980, which marked the end of what had been the *Destiny* tour. In spring 1981, the Jacksons readied themselves for a summer tour to promote the album; Michael was not happy about joining the tour because of the amount of time and preparation it would involve, especially as he was itching to get back to the recording studio to record the follow-up to *Off the Wall*. However, once he had committed, he threw himself wholeheartedly into the process.

A global press conference was called to alert the world to the forthcoming tour; attending the event, British journalist Mark Cooper noted how different Jackson was to his brothers. "Michael *is* a superstar," he wrote. "He looks and moves like a black Bambi, all grace and innocence, huge eyes and eyelashes and delicate Egyptian cheekbones. Astonishingly his voice is as high when he speaks as when he sings. He seems at once dependent on his brothers and off in a world of his own. He gushes with childlike enthusiasm and then loses interest, grows absent."[6]

The tour itself was an absolute, ahem, triumph; probably the greatest of the brothers' careers. Beginning in Memphis in September 1981, it gave a short, sharp blast of the Jacksons at their

most professional: a fourteen-song burst that incorporated the best of *Off the Wall*, *Triumph*, and *Destiny*, yet still making time for "Ben" and the early-hits medley. With a watertight band behind them—including stalwarts David Williams on guitar, Mike McKinney on bass, and Jonathan "Sugarfoot" Moffett on drums—and the Jacksons' immaculate showmanship, this was a memorable show. Their look was strong: wet perms, Jheri curls, and spangled outfits; they looked like a troupe of futuristic circus performers.

Jackson worked tirelessly to give the stage set a *Close Encounters* feel; magician Doug Henning worked with him to make him disappear into a puff of smoke at the end of "Don't Stop 'til You Get Enough." He was clear in his intent: with bands like Earth, Wind & Fire and the Commodores battling them for supremacy—the Jacksons felt they had to do something to counter the views of those who felt that they had "been around for ten years and were finished."[7]

A souvenir double live album was put together in time for Christmas 1981. *The Jacksons Live!* was released on November 11 and is a perfect capture of the group at a high watermark. It contains virtually all of the show, right down to the spoken-word section that reprised their lives to date. An in-concert version of the *Destiny* album track "Things I Do for You" was used as a single to promote the album. The cheers are noticeably louder for the *Off the Wall* tracks, nearing Jacksonmania again when "She's Out of My Life" is sung as it segues neatly from "This Place Hotel." The album's gatefold featured an onstage composite of the brothers, but the greatest image was

reserved for the reverse: Jackson on point in his patent loafers and sparkling white socks—the *Off the Wall* sleeve brought to life.

COMING-OF-AGE

Before all this, in August 1979, Michael Jackson turned twenty-one. It was around this time that he hired John Branca to represent him legally. A corporate tax lawyer with strong music industry connections, Branca seemed perfect for Jackson. He immediately renegotiated Jackson's CBS contract. A clause was also put in that would mean that Michael would be free to leave his brothers without jeopardizing their contract with the label.

This was exactly the sort of contract a man who was about to release the biggest-selling album in the history of popular music needed. It was around this time, too, that Jackson had his first bout of plastic surgery; a second followed during the *Triumph* rehearsals, making his nose, for which he had been so teased, even smaller.

OPPOSITE: *The* Jacksons Live *was a great double-album, capturing the brothers at their collective peak.*
ABOVE: *Reading all about it: Michael Jackson at home in Encino, California, 1981.*

The enormous success of Thriller *was a perfect storm of many things; remarkable tunes; world-class production; the stellar guests; the album's videos being shown incessantly around the world; the maturation of MTV; the globalization of record-company marketing; but most importantly, the advances made on an album he made in 1979 that captured him at the exact moment when he became an adult. That album was called* Off the Wall.

CHAPTER 11

KEEP ON WITH THE FORCE—DON'T STOP

THE SHEER DANCE-FLOOR OPULENCE OF OFF THE WALL

"I didn't want Off the Wall *to sound like outtakes from* Destiny*."*
—MICHAEL JACKSON[1]

I n 1979, it was certainly not a given that Michael Jackson would become an adult solo superstar. It was then nearly a decade since he and his brothers came blazing onto the scene, but the latter-day success of the Jacksons had been sizeable rather than spectacular. *Destiny* had indeed proved popular, but there were still those who believed that their move away from Motown had sounded a long, slow death-knell for them.

Off the Wall was to change all that. Michael Jackson's fifth solo album was released on August 10, 1979, on Epic Records. Arriving in the same month that he turned twenty-one, it was an amazing moment, presenting a new, seemingly fully formed Jackson to the wider world. "Shake Your Body (Down to the Ground)" from the previous year had hinted at the direction that he would be taking. Yet even the accomplishment of that slick piece could not have really prepared anyone for *this*. The first solo album to generate four US Top 10 hits, *Off the Wall* was a work that was to act as a full stop to the 1970s and an opening chapter for the new decade. Its advances in sonics, songwriting, and presentation showed that Jackson—and the new team behind him—had something truly potent to offer. As disco was becoming despised in the popular consciousness, here was a new, robust dance-pop that was seemingly future-proof.

OPPOSITE: *Jackson posing with his five* Billboard Magazine *awards for* Off The Wall. *In the future, a mere five awards would not be enough.*

ENTER QUINCY JONES

The genesis of *Off the Wall* starts back with *The Wiz*. The film had a very strong impact on Jackson. Although ultimately a commercial failure, it granted him a level of independence from his brothers. Here, he saw the machinations of showbiz as a maturing adult, standing on his own, not just as part of the collective. While working on the film, he consulted with Quincy Jones, the show's producer and musical director, about production ideas for his forthcoming solo album.

The pair had met briefly twice before, but this was the first significant time they worked together. "One day I called Quincy up to ask if he could suggest some great people who might want to do my album," Jackson told *Melody Maker* in 1980. "I was looking for somebody who would give me that freedom, plus somebody who's unlimited musically." Jones immediately put himself forward for the role.

"It sounded so phony," Jackson continued. "Like I was trying to hint to that—but I wasn't. I didn't even think of that. But Quincy does jazz, he does movie scores, rock 'n' roll, funk, pop—he's all colors, and that's the kind of people I like to work with. I went over to his house just about every other day, and we just put it together."[2]

Jones was indeed an apposite choice as producer. A pioneering African-American creative, he had been working in popular music since the early 1950s when, after graduating, he toured Europe as trumpeter with Lionel Hampton. Jones had gone on to write, produce, play, and

OPPOSITE: *Jackson in the studio, 1977; he wanted to learn as much as possible about recording techniques and encouraged his producers to incorporate his ideas.* RIGHT: *The dream team: Michael and Quincy, Los Angeles, 1979.*

Jackson clowns around as Charlie Chaplin, with Bruce Swedien and Quincy Jones.

arrange with some of the most legendary stars of the twentieth century, including Peggy Lee, Ella Fitzgerald, and Frank Sinatra. He had run Mercury Records and received Academy Award nominations for his film scores. What was most important, with all the various genres of music he had worked within over the preceding three decades, was that Jones had an extremely open mind. Yet it was still seen as a bold move by Jackson to enlist Jones to oversee this album, as his credentials as a contemporary pop-chart producer had yet to be fully tested. It was to mark the beginning of one of the most successful partnerships in popular music. What Jackson *was* clear about was that he was going to put himself in the center of a new lineup, using the best studios possible, alongside the finest writers and producers. As much as he loved his brothers, he didn't want to be recording with the old hierarchies hovering into view—and him being the butt of jokes—now that he was his own man.

With touring commitments, Jackson simply didn't have the time to write a full album of songs, and he desired Jones to A&R the best and most sympathetic material possible for him. (He was to write two and co-write another, as well as co-producing all three.) The overarching message was clear: Jackson wanted his fans to feel satisfied. The last thing he wanted was a Motown-style hits-and-fillers special. And he didn't want the album to sound like the Jacksons. "Hard words to spit out," he later wrote, "considering how hard we'd worked to become the Jacksons."[3]

Keyboard player Greg Phillinganes acted as music director (a role he had performed with élan on *Destiny*) and percussionist Paulinho da Costa returned as well to a lineup that contained some of the hottest players in Los Angeles. Jones had been working with the Brothers Johnson, and, as a result, Louis "Thunderthumbs" Johnson was to give the album its incredibly fluid bass drive. The album was to take around six months to record at Allen Zentz Recording in Hollywood, with strings added at Cherokee and horns recorded at Westlake, where Jones was ably assisted by his long-term engineer Bruce Swedien.

"DON'T STOP 'TIL YOU GET ENOUGH"

So much hinges around the majesty of the album's opening track and lead single, "Don't Stop 'til You Get Enough." The first song entirely written by Jackson became the foundation stone on which all of his future career would be built. The original idea came to him at the Jacksons' home in Encino. He could not stop bouncing the melody around his head, walking around singing and ad-libbing about faith and the power of love; immediately he and brother Randy went into their home studio and cut a demo on piano and percussion. The song was built around its loose, almost tribal groove, a groove that had been unlocked on "Shake Your Body (Down to the Ground)." Here the formula was notched up to its highest limit, creating something at once rooted in the soil and flying high in the galaxies.

Nineteen musicians made the noise that still sounds like the future, standing with Donna Summer's "I Feel Love" and Chic's "Le Freak" as one of the most monumental records of its age. With the first film of the *Star Wars* franchise

enjoying its tremendous global popularity, Jackson's choice of using the phrase "the force" was canny, placing him at the heart of the pop-culture *lingua franca*. With its propulsive, grinding beat, it became an enormous hit, reaching the top of the *Billboard* Hot 100 in October 1979.

No one else could have made this record. Although Jamaican reggae act Derrick Laro and Trinity did a lone, beautiful version of it at the time, it was impossible to emulate the original. Simply put, it was Jackson's; it could not have been anybody else's. It introduced his falsetto (then widely popular thanks to the Bee Gees) and also what was soon to become his gallery of trademark vocal tics. Take away the contemporaneous references to "the force," and you have something that is timeless; from its itching bass synth intro and Jackson's vocal explosion, it is one of the greatest side one, track one records ever.

ENTER ROD TEMPERTON . . . AND FRIENDS

With the halo effect of "Don't Stop" in place, *Off the Wall*'s smooth blend of Jackson originals and covers goes on to work seamlessly, nowhere more so than on the material by a man who would become synonymous with Jackson, writer and musician Rod Temperton, who had come to Quincy Jones' attention as the principal writer for UK-based Anglo-American disco

LEFT: *Jackson at his home, 1979.* OPPOSITE: *Rod Temperton's (right) writing brought a new dimension to Jackson's material, and provided him with some of his greatest songs.*

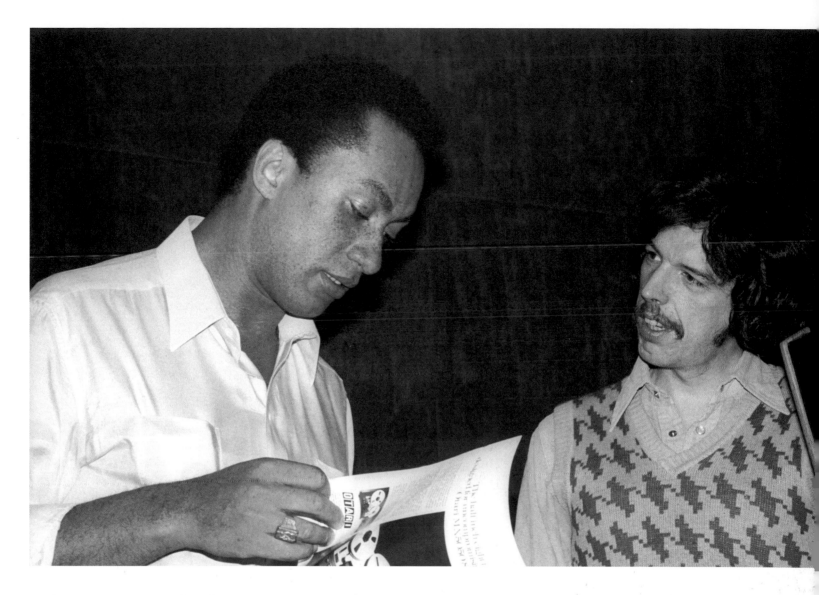

outfit Heatwave. His "Rock with You" was a key number. It had been penned originally as a frenetic dance song, yet Jackson softened the groove to create a wistfully dreamy piece of synth-pop. Jackson enjoyed Temperton's writing, and the two worked together successfully over this and what was to become his next album. Jackson liked the UK-born Temperton because, as he later wrote, "like me, he felt more at home singing and writing about the night life than actually going out and living it."[4] It was from

"Rock with You" that Temperton brought along two additional numbers, "Burn This Disco Out" and what went on to be the album's title track, "Off the Wall."

The sharp contrast offered between the first two tracks on the album ("Don't Stop" and "Rock with You") showcases the breadth of Jackson's material. "Rock with You" became his second US No. 1 from the album, reaching the top spot in January 1980, and remaining there for four weeks.

The album was initially to have been called "Girlfriend," after the Paul McCartney–penned song, which the Beatle had originally written with Jackson in mind. McCartney had subsequently released it on his own *London Town* album in 1978. By a strange quirk of fate, Quincy Jones suggested that Jackson cover the song as Jones thought it sounded perfect for him. It was one of several strange happenstances that drove the album forward.

Jackson was excited and nervous about the album's release. Speaking to *Blues and Soul* in August 1979 about the album's makeup, he said, "Stevie Wonder wrote a song and Paul McCartney wrote one. I wrote three songs and Louis Johnson wrote one. Quincy Jones produced it and we had a ball. It was the smoothest album I have ever been involved in. There was so much love, it was incredible. Everybody worked together so easily."[5] His friend Stevie had given him the gentle groove of "I Can't Help It," which helped get the album on FM radio stations.

The other standout ballad on the album is "She's Out of My Life." Written by former Jan and Dean songwriter Tom Bahler, the song highlights the increasing depth of Jackson as a singer. Jones had originally intended the song for Frank Sinatra, unsure if Jackson had the emotional gravitas to pull off such a heartbreaking song. It gave Jackson one of his most-loved performances, culminating in him crying at the end of the take, the lyrics having had such a striking effect on him. "I had been letting so much build up inside of me," he later wrote. "I was twenty-one years old, and I was so rich in some experiences while being poor in moments of true joy."[6]

LIFE AIN'T SO BAD AT ALL: REACTIONS TO OFF THE WALL

Perhaps the greatest revelation of *Off the Wall* was the sleeve itself. Designed by Mike Salisbury, it portrayed Jackson, standing, simply, in front of a wall. It was Salisbury's ideas for Steve Harvey's photography that captured the essence of this new Jackson. Salisbury wanted to combine the classic look of Frank Sinatra with Jackson's youthful exuberance. Last seen in the gatefold sleeve of *Destiny*, Jackson had been sporting an enormous Afro and an open-necked green satin smock top. Here, he is styling a simple tuxedo, with crisp white shirt and black bow tie. As the gatefold opens, it reveals the full cover, showing Jackson's legs with a glowing pair of white socks above his black patent leather shoes. It had been Jackson's idea to add the socks, and Salisbury suggested his trousers be raised so he could pay homage to another American icon, Gene Kelly.

ABOVE: *Jackson's shining disco moment, and still one of his most exciting releases:* Off the Wall. OPPOSITE: *The tuxedo-with-white-socks look defined Jackson's coming-of-age.*

Although Jackson had been a song-and-dance man right from the start of his career, here he was as a beautiful young man with the world at his feet, standing outside the stage door, ready to go on and knock 'em dead.

In the United States, the album was ironically kept off the top spot for much of its run by *The Wall* by Pink Floyd. In the UK, looking at the special relationship Jackson enjoyed with the country and how Britain had taken the Jackson 5 to their bosom, CBS was leaving little to chance to break its new

solo artist. Initial copies came complete with the picture disc of "You Can't Win" to further entice purchasers. Although it never rose higher than No. 5, *Off the Wall* spent 186 consecutive weeks—three and a half years—on the UK album chart, with its first four singles all hitting the Top 10.

Off the Wall unlocked not only the potential of Jackson but also the importance of shrewd, widespread marketing to the world. The final singles were being pulled off the album nearly a year after release. As Elvis Presley had let his films tour the world for him, Jackson could harness the promo clip and let it do the same for him. The bringing to life of the album's cover, albeit with a bigger bow tie, in the Nick Saxton–directed video for "Don't Stop 'til You Get Enough," saw audiences marvel as Jackson triplicated himself onscreen.

Off the Wall continued to sell, and unceasingly gained new fans. Reviewers contemporaneously and subsequently have listened to the album in slack-jawed wonder. This truly was a sound like little else. It was, as the *NME* opined, "A cross-Atlantic, multiracial, dance-floor hedonist's manifesto . . . a truly explosive sound: a peak of achievement which others had to aim for."[7]

Off the Wall went on to sell over twenty million copies worldwide. It is revered by critics, as illustrated by UK writer David Stubbs, who said in *Uncut* magazine in 2001 that it contained "the neon-lit sublimity of the title track, 'Don't Stop 'til You Get Enough,' with its fountainous orchestral backdrop and overspill of wordless whoops,' the brassy, accelerated ecstasy of 'Working Day and Night' and 'Get on the Floor'—wooo!"[8] Jackson had managed to come of age without the explicit involvement of his family. A cursory glance at the credits finds a single solitary brother listed. And that brother was Randy, the one he cut the early demo of "Don't Stop" with, the one younger than him, whom he could tease.

Off the Wall was the end of an era. As Gavin Martin pointed out in *NME* in 1982, "It was the final summation of the great disco party, one long last fling before conscience, art and politics became features on the horizon,"[9] but what an all-singing, all dancing way to go. It was also the beginning of a new phase. If the Jackson 5 mania had been the trailer, the main feature of Jackson's stardom was to begin right here.

The album was nominated for two Grammy awards yet won only one, for "Best Male Vocal R&B Performance." Jackson was furious. He felt ignored by his peers and told CBS boss Walter Yentnikoff that he wanted more.

Yentnikoff picks up the story with his response in his autobiography, *Howling at the Moon*:

" 'Make more records and you'll get more Grammys.'

" 'My next record will win every Grammy there is.'

" 'From your mouth to God's ear.'

"Turned out God was listening."[10]

OPPOSITE: *Jackson receiving an award from Leif Garrett and Chuck Berry at the American Music Awards, 1980.* ABOVE: *A beautiful young man with the world at his feet: Jackson in the early 1980s.*

The breakout success of Off the Wall *had been incubating for a considerable period. Its funky, propulsive roots can be traced back to the Jackson 5's late Motown success with "Dancing Machine" in 1974, which really seemed to relocate the brothers to the dance floor. The next period would be one of new opportunities and thrilling constant change after the Jacksons did the unthinkable: left Motown.*

CHAPTER 12

GOIN' PLACES
LIFE AFTER MOTOWN

"We're really excited about it because we wrote and produced it all ourselves and it's the first time we've done that."

—MICHAEL JACKSON, 1978[1]

It took some time for the Jacksons to deliver new material. The Motown contract officially expired on March 10, 1976: live engagements, including a brief tour to the Philippines (six dates in Manila) had to be honored but, for the first time, it felt like the group had sufficient time to complete the work that was being asked of them.

Jackson Sr. had lined up a new TV series for them with CBS TV. Michael Jackson did not wish to participate, but the early episodes of the series—based broadly on the group's Las Vegas revue—were a hit, and more episodes were ordered. A mixture of sketches and songs, as was the wont of the era, it also featured documentary sequences showing a pensive Michael at the family's Hayvenhurst mansion. The series brought all of the children together (except Jermaine, who seemed as if he no longer existed) and was a classic slice of mid-'70s TV gold, with guest performers across the twelve episodes ranging from Sonny Bono to Muhammad Ali and Wonder Woman's Lynda Carter. Directed by Bill Davis, the brothers and sisters would sing up to six songs per episode with their guests. It was the first primetime US TV show where all the main performers were not only siblings but also an African-American family. Jackson felt the TV show was a "dumb move," however, and "hated every minute of it."[2]

It was time for the group to return to the studio. One of the most interesting moves of the '70s was to see the Jacksons freed from one production treadmill and put on another: the group was assigned to the legendary Philadelphia International Records, part of the Epic/Columbia family, which had been founded in 1971 by writers and producers Kenny Gamble and Leon Huff. The brothers would be on the roster alongside Harold Melvin and the

OPPOSITE: *Jackson doing one of his favorite things: listening to music.*

Bluenotes, the O'Jays, and Phyllis Hyman. The change certainly suited them.

Recorded in Philadelphia, the first (self-titled) Jacksons album was released in November 1976, and it brought the might of PIR to the Jacksons' world. Everything was more sophisticated: the strings were as intricate and complex as you would expect; the Sigma Sound recording studio band, MFSB (Mother-Father-Sister-Brother), lent the record its trademark urban lushness. Of the ten tracks, Huff and Gamble wrote half. The other house writers were involved, too: Dexter Wansel, Victor Carstarphen, Gene McFadden, and John Whitehead.

However, the album was significant for allowing the group to contribute their own material, one of the key tenets that Joe Jackson had brokered in the Epic deal. "Blues Away" is one of the most significant tracks in the entire Michael Jackson catalogue—his first published song, written on his own. Also, at 1:16 we first hear the stuttering, gasping vocal style, which would later so become his trademark. It's a slight song, but it was *his* song. Written by Michael with Tito, "Style of Life" was the album's other original. It wasn't great, but again, it was theirs. Once more, Jackson drank in the work of experienced studio hands: "Just watching Huff play the piano while Gamble sang taught me more about the anatomy of a song than anything else . . . I'd sit there like a hawk, observing every decision, listening to every note."[3]

The album's lead single, "Enjoy Yourself," an upbeat call to action, reached No. 6 in the US charts and gave them their first significant hit in years. Another important thing about the sleeve

of the album, a treated and colorized Norman Seeff portrait of the group, was that it fully located, arguably for the first time, their blackness, and they were all laughing, naturally, as if to say, "We are delighted with our new home." Although it only reached No. 28 in the United States, the single "Show You the Way to Go" became an enormous hit in the UK, surprising Epic. It reached No. 1 for a week before the Queen's Silver Jubilee celebration in 1977 and soundtracked that hot summer of punk rock. Epic got the brothers on a plane and they appeared on UK pop show *Top of the Pops* and at a special Royal Command Performance in Glasgow, where they sang in front of Queen Elizabeth II. In retrospect, "Show You the Way to Go" seems a peculiar smash hit in all its mid-tempo mellowness. But it clearly signified that the Jacksons had grown up and were ready for business. It also offered the group its first-ever gold record for album sales. It is said that Jackson was bitterly disappointed, though, as he thought the album was on its way to platinum sales.

GOIN' PLACES

The Jacksons' second album for PIR, *Goin' Places*, released in October 1977, was something of a misstep. It seemed dated. "There were more songs with messages and not as many dance songs," Jackson was later to write. "We knew that the message to promote peace and let music take over was a good one, but [it was] not our style."[4]

The public was not particularly interested in the album, but the two group self-writes showed great promise. "Different Kind of Lady" shows

OPPOSITE: *Happy together? A promotional picture for the short-lived CBS TV show* The Jacksons.

ABOVE: *The Jacksons perform on* The Tonight Show, *June 1976.* LEFT: The Jacksons live at London's Hammersmith Odeon, 1977. OPPOSITE: Goin' Places *failed to ignite in the same way their first album for CBS had.*

THE JACKSONS   GOIN' PLACES

what the Jacksons wanted to do; it is probably the greatest hit the brothers never had. The swing-boogie of their other song "Do What You Wanna" is again streets ahead of the other material, and sounds as if the brothers were fully engaged with what they were singing.

Elsewhere, "Heaven Knows I Love You, Girl" is like a Harold Melvin and the Bluenotes outtake, and it just sounds uncomfortable for the brothers to be singing it. Working with Gamble and Huff had been an incredible experience for the brothers, but *Goin' Places* demonstrated that the union was reaching its natural end. It became one of the group's lowest-selling releases of all, only reaching No. 52 on *Billboard*'s Top 100. Besides, with their growing confidence, and the fact that the four songs they had written across the last two records had gained considerable plaudits, it was time for the Jacksons really to strike out.

Michael went with his father to see CBS's Alexenberg, to ask to be able to go it alone for the next album. Ironically, prior to the meeting,

much behind-the-scenes maneuvering had been going on. New president Yetnikoff was considering dropping the group altogether, as the sales for both albums had not been great. It was West Coast artist-relations manager Bobby Colomby who convinced Alexenberg and Yetnikoff to give the group another try. At the meeting, Alexenberg agreed to the father and son's demands.

THE WIZ

Michael Jackson got his wish to move into films with *The Wiz*, which began filming in New York in October 1977. Written by Charlie Smalls and William F. Brown, the stage musical, an African-American adaptation of L. Frank Baum's *The Wizard of Oz* (*The Wiz: The Super Soul Musical "Wonderful Wizard of Oz"* to give it its full title) had opened in Baltimore in 1974, before moving to Broadway's Majestic Theater in January 1975. After a shaky start, it became a huge hit, winning seven Tony Awards, and brought singer Stephanie Mills to the world's attention.

Berry Gordy bought the film rights to *The Wiz* for Motown, in partnership with Universal. Working with young producer Rob Cohen, who had produced *Mahogany* for Gordy, Mills was signed to re-create her Broadway role of Dorothy, in what was to be an earthy, low-budget production, along the lines of the enormous breakout success *Car Wash*, a couple of years previously. However, that was to change when Diana Ross began campaigning for the role. Gordy disagreed vehemently with her, suggesting that, at thirty-three, she was simply too old for the role. Ross disagreed and went directly to producer Cohen. Ross was

ABOVE: *The Jacksons launch* Goin' Places, *July 1977.* OPPOSITE: *Working on the soundtrack of* The Wiz *with Diana Ross, 1978.*

undeniably a much bigger star, yet she was not the twelve-year-old child Dorothy.

This choice would provide one of the principal pieces of criticism leveled against the film. The director originally assigned to the film, John Badham, withdrew and retreated to make *Saturday Night Fever* instead. When Ross heard that Jackson was being considered for the role of the scarecrow, she lobbied for him: "I was enthusiastic," she later wrote. "I thought it would be wonderful for Michael and me to work together . . . even though this would be Michael's very first acting role, I told them that I considered him an ideal choice."[5]

Jackson was in, and would bring a tremendous exuberance to the role. He was working with some of the very best in the business: director Sidney Lumet was probably at his greatest after a run of huge successes such as *The Anderson Tapes*, *Dog Day Afternoon*, *Serpico*, and *Network*, and writer Joel Schumacher was the go-to guy for scripts. Shooting would take place in New York, where Jackson relocated with his sister LaToya, living apart from his family for the first time. The pair lived in a thirty-seventh-floor apartment at Manhattan's select Sutton Place. It provided him with an incredible opportunity to sample some of the New York lifestyle; he would become a visitor to Studio 54, often with Ross. Here, his mind would be opened to the new sounds and styles that were reshaping disco music.

Jackson recalled the entire experience with considerable affection. Filming took place at Astoria Studios in Queens (where *Sesame Street* was shot) and ran through until the end of December 1977. Jackson was incredibly focused on his work, including the five hours a day it took to put on his makeup (as he was worried about

his complexion, being buried in a mask suited him), and then looked forward to the nightlife. He would never feel so free again.

The Wiz would finally be released on October 26, 1978; although it lost money from its $24 million budget and garnered some truly terrible reviews, it had an enormous impact on the African-American community—and more importantly, an enormous impact on Michael Jackson himself. He was one of the few people on

the whole film to emerge unscathed. Here he was, on his own, truly standing apart from his brothers. He had performed strongly in his solo song, "You Can't Win," which had been written by Charlie Smalls solely for him in the film, and the discipline of moviemaking would be something that he would bring into his later promotional videos.

Most importantly, Michael Jackson was able to ask the film's music producer, Quincy Jones, a significant question: would he be interested in producing his next solo record, his first for Epic? Jones was smitten with Jackson at the time: he told UK magazine *Blues and Soul* that "Michael Jackson . . . is the epitome of a natural actor. Scenes that take seasoned veterans a while to pull off, Michael does in one take. The kid is going to be a major motion picture star, and this movie is going to let everyone know."[6]

PEACOCK PRODUCTIONS

After filming finished, Jackson went straight back to pick up with his brothers. It was imperative that if the Jacksons were to succeed, they move forward on their own terms. This was the beginning of their freedom. Working with Gamble and Huff had been a blast, properly collaborative, but they needed to strike out on their own. The group had decided to form its own production company and was searching for titles for the enterprise. Michael read an article on peacocks in a newspaper and remembered with joy the one Berry Gordy had at one of his homes. In the piece, he read that the peacock's full plumage would "explode" in all the colors of the rainbow—but only when the peacock was in love. This image clearly struck a chord with him; the logo would appear on the group's future albums.

Around the same time, Joe Jackson appointed Ron Weisner and Freddy DeMann as the group's managers. Both were experienced industry men, and Joe felt they had sufficient gravitas to ensure that CBS gave his boys due care and attention. The Jacksons would have their own company within CBS, and would establish themselves as writers, producers, and arrangers as well as artists. CBS stipulated that the group would need an A&R man, too, and assigned Bobby Colomby to the role. Colomby suggested the young keyboard player Greg Phillinganes as their arranger. This was to be the real beginning of the Jacksons' period at CBS. The first bit of business for the

OPPOSITE TOP: *Michael with older sister LaToya at home in 1977.* OPPOSITE BOTTOM: *Jackson's performance as the scarecrow is one of the best things about* The Wiz. ABOVE: *Jackson dancing with Diana Ross at the premiere of* The Wiz *at Studio 54, 1978.*

brothers was to attend to their *Goin' Places* tour between January and May; in between shows and straight afterward, they headed to the studio.

DESTINY

Epic finally received a proper return on its investment with the Jacksons' third album for the label. Moving from the PIR imprint to Epic itself, *Destiny* marked the Jacksons' coming-of-age. Released in time for Christmas 1978, it became a four-million-selling album worldwide.

Michael Jackson was clearly keyed-up in interviews in 1978. He and his brothers were enjoying their independence. "We have a new album called *Destiny* coming out in November," he told the UK's *Record Mirror*, "which we're really excited about because we wrote and produced it all ourselves and it's the first time we've done that." He added that he had written three of the tracks with Randy: "All Night Dancin'," "That's What You Get," and "Shake Your Body (Down to the Ground)," which he described as "really long, like eight minutes, and really in the groove."[7]

Recorded at a variety of studios on the West Coast of America, *Destiny* was a bright, confident album, sounding very much like a new beginning for the group. Bobby Colomby was proving an excellent ally: as well as bringing in Phillinganes to arrange, he had also suggested percussionist Paulinho da Costa to fill out the sound. If that was not enough, he brought the group the album's lead single, and, ultimately, the only outside songwriting contribution to the album. Unbelievably, this track, "Blame It on the Boogie," was written by a British singer born Michael Jackson (but known as Mick). His own version competed with the Jacksons' when it was released in the UK in 1978. It was a jaunty opener for the new album, and it allowed the group to says that all the songs were written by people called "Jackson."

The album offers all the light and shade of a Jacksons album, with a new, unified sound—no more Philly house producers or Motown production line. The tracks range from the good time party of "Things I Do for You" to the lush, beautiful balladry of "Push Me Away" to the Commodores-influenced country-soul of the title track. However, everything is dwarfed by "Shake Your Body (Down to the Ground)," one of those truly incredible records that only Michael Jackson could create. He did this four or five

ABOVE: *Where the Jacksons story REALLY begins:* Destiny, *the album that set the template for Michael's solo superstardom.* OPPOSITE: *The Jacksons in their stage costumes, ready to perform in 1978.*

times in his career. Three were based on similar grooves—"Don't Stop 'til You Get Enough," "Jam," and "Wanna Be Startin' Somethin' " are notable examples. It could be said that Jackson truly found his voice here, with his breathy falsetto—inspired in part by the Bee Gees.

Written by Randy and Michael, "Shake Your Body (Down to the Ground)" was the first time they truly married disco rhythms with something more visceral, a return-to-Africa rhythm that nodded to Lamont Dozier's nine-minute opus "Going Back to My Roots" from his 1977 album *Peddlin' Music on the Side* (which in turn had been influenced by Alex Haley's groundbreaking 1976 novel *Roots: The Saga of an American Family*). Inspired partially by the ad libs from Marvin Gaye's "Got to Give It Up" from the previous year and the groove of Teddy's Pendergrass' "Get Up, Get Down, Get Funky, Get Loose," the single would become a cornerstone of future live performances and reached the Top 10 on both sides of the Atlantic.

Taking a leaf out of labelmates Earth, Wind & Fire's book, everything about *Destiny* seemed bigger, bolder, more mythic, from the gatefold sleeve art inward. These were not brothers getting down in a city; these were brothers on top of a stone monolith, in stormy seas, with a vortex cyclone behind them as lighting strikes, awaiting their destiny.

And on the reverse, through the beautiful fanned tail of the peacock, is a message written by Michael and Jackie, stating where they were at. "Through the ages, the peacock has been honored and praised for its attractive, illustrious beauty. Of all the bird family, the peacock is the only bird that integrates all colors into one, and displays this radiance of fire only when in love. We, like the peacock, try to integrate all races into one through the love of music."

Destiny leaps out at you: it is the Jacksons' truly fanning their tails, finally relocating the zest and the joy of their music and running freely. This joyous freedom encapsulated so succinctly by his brothers was only the beginning. Now it was time for Michael Jackson to go truly off the wall . . .

The move of Michael Jackson and his brothers to CBS would have enormous ramifications for the group. But before the relationship with Motown was to sour, Berry Gordy and Joe Jackson made a decision that proved extremely prescient: to allow Michael to run his own solo career alongside the group. Modeled very much as a forlorn teen crooner, Jackson, then thirteen, began to amass a great deal of fans who wished only to see him.

CHAPTER 13

"I" AND "ME"
FROM FIRST SOLO STEPS TO ROBOT DANCING

"It was a boy who befriended a rat. People didn't understand the boy's love for this little creature. He was dying of some disease and his only true friend was Ben, the leader of the rats in the city where they lived. A lot of people thought the movie was a bit odd. but I was not one of them."

—MICHAEL JACKSON[1]

GOT TO BE THERE

Toward the end of the crazed year of 1971, Michael Jackson released his first solo single. Inspired by the solo success that Donny Osmond was having while still a member of the Osmonds, Joe Jackson and Berry Gordy felt that Michael should begin a concurrent, standalone career. They would later suggest the same for Jermaine. Recorded at Hitsville West, Michael Jackson's first single, "Got to Be There," was written by Elliot Willensky and produced by Hal Davis. It had originally been intended for the brothers, but Gordy felt this was the right track with which to begin Michael's solo career. It was a huge success reminiscent of the Jackson 5's "I'll Be There," almost taking the "look over your shoulder, honey" line and building his early Motown career on it. By November 1971, the record was in the Top Five on both sides of the Atlantic.

When the first Michael Jackson album, *Got to Be There*, was released in January 1972, it contained nine further variants of the title track. Jackson was photographed by Jim Britt for the album's sleeve and appears relaxed and smiling, wearing an oversized cap (which he wanted to wear to sing the title track onstage). It was clear that with

OPPOSITE: *Jackson performing at the Inglewood Forum, California, August 26, 1973.*

ABOVE: *Jim Britt's photo of Jackson in his oversized cap defined him in his first phase as a solo artist.*
OPPOSITE: *Jackson in 1972—not yet fourteen years old, but with almost a decade of show-business experience behind him.*

this album, Michael was being set up as a teenage voice for millions of girls to identity with the world over—a shoulder to cry on, if you will. It was a part he played extremely convincingly. He would work quickly to create this pathos: as Suzee Ikeda, his vocal coach and one of his key mentors at Motown, recalled, "He had the quickest ears of anybody. No one showed him that level of creativity. That was him, his soul."[2]

Recorded between June and November 1971 and produced by Hal Davis, Willie Hutch, and the Corporation™, the album's many highlights included two contemporary covers: his version of Bill Withers' "Ain't No Sunshine" and Carole King's "You've Got a Friend." But it was not all downbeat—his cover of Bobby Day's old '50s hit "Rockin' Robin" adds youthful zest to the R&B number, reaching the Top 3 in the United States and UK—and it was clear that he was very much a force be reckoned with on his own. Michael was the epitome of your teenage friend, growing up alongside his audience.

LOOKIN' THROUGH THE WINDOWS AND BEN

There was little time for Jackson to savor his solo success, as it was back to Jackson 5 business. Although the group's career was settling down from its accelerated Motown beginning, their albums continued to be a shop window for the best writers in the Motown stable. Released in May 1972, *Lookin' Through the Windows* found the group tackling more adult material, and also, importantly marked the beginning of Jackson's maturation into a tenor rather than the soprano of his early work. Clifton Davis, who supplied "Never Can Say Goodbye" for the *Third Album*, provided the album's title track, another reflection on life and love. A cover of Thurston Harris' "Little Bitty Pretty One" finds the collected brothers looking for a little of the success of "Rockin' Robin," while the inspired selection of Jackson Browne's "Doctor My Eyes" demonstrated that the group could handle material away from what may be deemed conventional boy-band territory. The album reached No. 7 on the United States charts.

Released in August 1972, "Ben" was to become Michael Jackson's biggest solo Motown hit, and introduced his second solo album to the world. Written by veteran film composer Don Black and Walter Scharf, it was, and remains, an odd record: a fifteen-year-old boy singing a love song to a rat. It was the theme song to the motion picture of the same name, itself the follow-up to the 1971 breakout US hit picture *Willard*, where rats begin to engulf their owner's residence and the titular rodent leads the charge. Jackson's is a beautifully fragile, tender performance, sweetly orchestrated. Were you

the Stylistics the previous year. "Everybody Is Somebody's Fool," made famous by Jimmy Scott, was earmarked to be the follow-up single from the album, but its release was canceled due to the lasting success of "Ben" and the splendidly upbeat "Greatest Show on Earth." Although the album didn't have the lasting success of its predecessor, *Ben* reached the US Top 20 and proved that Jackson was now established as a solo performer.

BY ROYAL COMMAND

In November 1972, the Jackson 5 undertook their first tour outside the United States, with eight concerts scheduled in Amsterdam, Paris, Munich, Brussels, and Frankfurt, plus UK gigs in London (at the prestigious Empire Pool Wembley), Liverpool, Manchester, and Birmingham. By this point, youngest brother Randy, now aged eleven, had joined the touring group on bongos. If there were any doubts about how they would be received, they were quickly quelled by the reaction of British audiences. With their familiarity guaranteed by their promotional videos and cartoon TV series, when the brothers arrived in the UK, Jacksonmania was ready to roll. The UK, which had been under the full thrall of Osmondmania for the best part of a year, was ready and waiting for the group. Motown took out full-page ads in the music papers: "Jackson 5ive Are Coming." Both "Lookin' Through the Windows" and "Ben" were being released for them to promote. Fans were waiting at the airport, screaming, in scenes that recalled the Beatles' arrivals just under a decade earlier. As the Motown press release stated, "It was near chaos. It was frightening. It was JACKSONMANIA."[3]

not aware of the subject matter, it could be a simple song of friendship, delightfully delivered.

In one of the Corporation™'s final productions for him, "Ben" gave him his first US No. 1 solo single, sitting at the top of the charts for a week that October. "Ben" is a tender song that captured the imagination and sold 1.7 million copies in the United States alone. It could be argued that Jackson went truly stratospheric when he sang the song at the Academy Awards ceremony the following March. Introduced by Charlton Heston, he charmed the Dorothy Chandler Pavilion and the global audience with his heartfelt performance. Although the song lost out at the ceremony to "The Morning After" by Maureen MacGovern, Michael Jackson as a solo performer was etched in the minds of many who would not be familiar with pop radio.

The parent album, *Ben*, was another collection of lovelorn ballads and mid-tempo steppers; also notable is Jackson's version of Thom Bell and Linda Creed's socially conscious "People Make the World Go Round," which had been a hit for

OPPOSITE: The Jacksons looking pensive on the sleeve of their 1972 album, Lookin' Through the Windows. ABOVE: Within a decade of this photo, Jackson would truly be in the deep end, at home, 1972. FAR LEFT: Jackson's most successful Motown solo album: Ben. LEFT: The brothers' delight is there for all to see on the sleeve of their debut CBS album, The Jacksons.

On October 30, the group performed at the Royal Variety Performance at the Palladium in London. It was one of those prestigious show-business events in the UK calendar, with Queen Elizabeth, the Queen Mother, in attendance. In a country that, at that point, had only three television channels and four radio stations, pop music was strictly rationed—there was *Top of the Pops*, a weekly program. The Royal Variety Performance—on which the Jackson 5 shared the bill with Elton John, Liberace, and Carol Channing—was broadcast on primetime TV just over a week later. It showed clearly that the Jacksons were no novelty act: despite their tender years, they were a

working band with a lot of road behind them; with three years of hits in the bag already, there was, as Michael later wrote, "enough to please."[4] With his tutor out there on tour with him, Jackson drank in all there was to see, getting more education from places and people than he would from books.

GETTING IT TOGETHER?

The year 1973 was largely defined by the brothers being on tour and recording and releasing albums in between. Their world tour would run intermittently through to 1975, taking in a variety of countries, all ready and willing to embrace

OPPOSITE: *The Jacksons arriving in London, October 1972.* ABOVE: *Michael and Randy onstage in London, 1972.*

the Jackson magic. As a result, it seemed that their next releases were almost afterthoughts. Michael Jackson's third album, *Music & Me*, was transitional; the cover shows him looking pensive with an acoustic guitar, but while he wanted to write his own material, Motown forbade him to do so. The album contains some lovely, tender ballads, including a version of "Happy," the love ballad from *Lady Sings the Blues*, and Stevie Wonder's "With a Child's Heart." However, the album seemed to be overlooked—especially

when, just a month or so later, the Jackson 5 returned with *Skywriter*.

By the time of *Skywriter*, the brothers were feeling alienated by the Motown setup. They were desperate to provide their own material but instead were now recording random tracks with a variety of producers. Their sales, although respectable by the standards of other groups, were declining. Joe Jackson was becoming irate that Berry Gordy was spending less time with his artists now that he was wrapped up in his

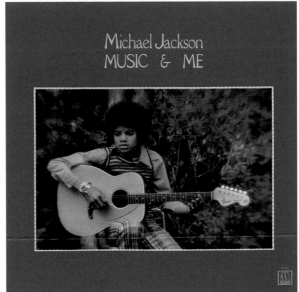

LEFT: *The Jackson 5's Royal Variety Performance gave them a new level of success in the UK.* TOP: *The transitional* Music and Me *album catches Jackson between child and adult.* ABOVE: *The sepia-toned biplane sleeve for 1973's* Skywriter *album.*

filmmaking. Ewart Abner was running the day-to-day business of the company and seemed less enamored with the brothers. The brothers looked glum by the wings of a biplane on the cover of their eighth album, which of course took a literal approach to the album's title, but these were no World War I flying aces. There was plenty to

ABOVE: G.I.T.—Get It Together *was an attempt to break away from the formula, especially the song "Dancing Machine."*
OPPOSITE: *Rehearsal backstage at the Inglewood Forum, California, August 26, 1973.*

enjoy, however: the title track gave them a Top 30 UK hit; a cover of the Supremes' "Touch" suggested sexual maturity; and "Hallelujah Day" featured great vocal interplay between the brothers. But with the group busy on tour and little time given over to promotion, *Skywriter* became the Jackson 5's lowest-selling album.

Recorded sporadically throughout 1973, the next Jackson 5 album, *G.I.T.—Get It Together*, was much more like it. Showing definite signs of progression, its eight songs, produced by Hal Davis and Norman Whitfield, were sequenced into two long dance tracks, one per side. Finally all of the brothers took lead vocal duties. One of the album's centerpieces is "Hum Along and Dance," which takes the old Temptations song and makes it funkier. It is interesting to hear the brothers finally given their own eight-minute track on which to stretch out. *G.I.T.* is an accomplished album, and it arrived just at the right time, but it showed that in one sense the group was in a state

of flux, finding it difficult to grow into the adult material that peers such as the Temptations could perform so effortlessly.

By 1973, Joe Jackson sensed that Motown was not giving the Jacksons the room they deserved, so he took the strange step of devising a Jackson family nightclub act, which was to play out across the United States. The act that was doing the rounds was seen later at Westbury Music Fair by the group's future CBS president, Walter Yetnikoff. He was less than impressed: "Their baby sister, who did a Mae West impression, looked silly. Their dance steps looked tired. The bright spot, of course, was sixteen-year-old Michael, who was lit from within."[5]

The year 1974 was another one of flux for the brothers. Still touring—the African leg of their world tour in February would have a profound effect on them—they embarked upon a more showbiz path, while enjoying one of their biggest late-period Motown hits. Written by Hal Davis, Don Fletcher, Dean Parks, "Dancing Machine" was the final track on *G.I.T.—Get It Together*. The song had been picked up by radio and became a breakout success as the disco movement began to take hold on the US underground. A performance of "Dancing Machine" on *Soul Train* in November 1973 propelled the song, when released as a single in February, to No. 2 in the United States, making it their first Top 10 hit since 1971. It was an astonishing performance, ahead of its time, and, as Jackson later wrote, "a lesson to me in the power of television . . . within a few days it seemed that every kid in the United States was doing the robot."[6]

On April 7, 1974, the Jacksons' show took up a residency at the MGM Grand, Las Vegas.

The show ran through to the 24th of the month and offered Joe Jackson a lucrative route map, were their recording career to slow down significantly. Adrian Grant, writing in *Michael Jackson, A Visual Documentary*, sums the shows up succinctly: "The shows are a big hit with fans, breaking attendance records, but receive a critical pounding."[7] Jackson liked the relative lack of pressure of cabaret, as opposed to the demands of a concert performance. The show was to return at the end of August.

The summer saw the group touring further (including a visit to South America in September) while recording with Stevie Wonder, adding backing vocals to his anti–Richard Nixon US No. 1 "You Haven't Done Nothin'." More material was

recorded, yet none of it made it to the brothers' next album. The success of "Dancing Machine" led to the last track of *G.I.T.–Get It Together* appearing again on the brothers' new album, also called *Dancing Machine*. Overseen solely by Hal Davis, it was released in September. It sees the group go disco: nine tracks with their eyes firmly on the floor. "I Am Love" and "Whatever You Got I Want" were credible singles that performed well on the R&B charts, and "If I Don't Love You This Way" and "What You Don't Know" were two of Jackson's personal favorites. The album went to No. 16 in the US charts, yet failed to register with UK audiences.

MOVING VIOLATION

Michael Jackson's final solo album for Motown was *Forever, Michael*. Released in January 1975, right as the very future of the Jackson 5 at Motown was being considered by Joe Jackson, the album was a credible capture of Jackson at seventeen. As historian Mark Anthony Neal notes, the album "didn't zoom up the pop charts, but was well accepted by black radio."[8] It contains a beautiful version of "We're Almost There," "Just a Little Bit of You," and the tender "One Day in Your Life," which would become a UK No. 1 single when released in 1981 in the wake of Jackson's later success.

What Jackson and his brothers wanted, however, was some more success *now*. They were simply not satisfied with the situation at Motown, and, led by father Joseph, they sensed that their days were numbered. Their twelfth and final album for the label, *Moving Violation*, was released on May 15, 1975. Again, in the wake of the success of "Dancing Machine," it certainly had an eye on the dance floor. It was assembled

OPPOSITE: *Jackson and Donny Osmond present former Motown president Ewart Abner with an American Music Award, 1974.* TOP: *The success of the track from G.I.T. prompted a whole album of dance confections.* ABOVE: *Forever, Michael is an assured snapshot of a maturing artist.*

by three different production teams: Brian Holland for Holland-Dozier-Holland Inc. (marking one of their first returns to Motown since their much-vaunted departure in 1968); Hal Davis; and Mel Larson and Jerry Marcellino. The brothers were dissatisfied with the disparity of styles and wished for consistency across the album.

The Holland-produced, James Carmichael–arranged "Honey Love" is generic disco; "Body Language (Do the Love Dance)" certainly has a swing to it, with plenty of in-era calls to "express yourself" and a nagging funk backing. The album was led by the single "Forever Came Today," a reworking of the 1968 song by the Supremes that sees Holland delve back into the H-D-H songbook; its B-side, "All I Do Is Think of You," also showed a strong performance. It became the last charting Jackson 5 single for Motown. With its stylized sleeve of the brothers running down a (white) traffic policeman in a huge, sleek, vintage automobile, *Moving Violation* sold around one-and-a-half-million worldwide. If that sleeve—an African-American group in a hugely expensive car bringing down the very establishment—had contained a record by, say, Funkadelic, or Sly and the Family Stone, it would have been seen as positively incendiary. Instead, it was mostly regarded—if it was seen at all—as somewhat comical. This was how irrelevant the Jackson 5 seemed at the halfway mark of the '70s.

GOING PLACES

It was getting too much for the core of the Jacksons; they could see that their popularity was waning, and they were caught in a slipstream at Motown, where they were frustrated not to be making the bold "adult" albums of Stevie Wonder (*Talking Book, Innervisions*) or Marvin Gaye (*What's Going On, Let's Get It On*), or being featured as a filmmaking superstar like Diana Ross. As a result, they seemed to be neither one thing nor another. Although they were far from the doldrums, there was a very real feeling that the group could soon be over. They were not allowed to be musical auteurs or thought of in the same breath as the greats, and they were on the verge of becoming that most toxic commodity in the music industry: the recently over phenomenon.

As 1975 progressed, the Jacksons made it clear they wanted greater artistic control with their releases, and a rise in their paltry 2.8 percent royalty rate. Joe Jackson looked to take the group's contract elsewhere. The word was out that they wanted to leave, and there was no shortage of interest. Industry grandee Jerry Wexler was very keen to sign them to Atlantic (an offshoot of which, Atco, had distributed the group's debut single, "Big Boy," for Steeltown all the way back in 1968), and there was a deal on the table for a million dollars, which ultimately was withdrawn.

Epic Records, an offshoot of the first US record company, Columbia, was ready to make the deal. New president Walter Yetnikoff and executive Ron Alexenburg were instrumental in getting the group on the label—and, at the time, it was not an absolute sure bet to get them signed. They were

OPPOSITE: *The group's final Motown album, Moving Violation.* ABOVE: *A late-period Motown press shot of the brothers; it was soon time to be goin' places.*

to become Yetnikoff's first signing, but that said, he had needed some convincing. "In my new role, wouldn't I be a schmuck to authorize a multi-million dollar deal to a guy pouring his heart out to a dead rat?"[9]

The move was to create a rift within the group as Jermaine Jackson was by now married to Hazel Gordy, Motown label founder Berry Gordy's daughter. Jermaine had little option but to stay with the label. After a contract-fulfilling concert in Las Vegas in May, Jermaine left the group, to be replaced by younger brother Randy. Family was family and business was business. Initially, Gordy wasn't overly concerned: the group was past its zenith and he was making his films. But this stance was soon to change.

On June 30, 1975, Joe Jackson announced at a press conference at Manhattan's Rainbow Grill on the roof of the Rockefeller Center that his sons—bar Jermaine—were signing with Epic. The Motown landscape shifted quickly. Vice-president Michael Roshkind was going to make it difficult, however: the name "Jackson 5" was trademarked to Motown. And so the Jackson 5 became the Jacksons. Gordy then filed a $5 million lawsuit for breach of contract, insisting that the group should not have signed elsewhere before the deal expired in 1976, and that a final album was owed. Joe Jackson countersued, suggesting that Motown owed them money. Gordy retaliated, saying that Joe Jackson owed him

Jermaine Jackson and Hazel Gordy on their wedding day, December 15, 1973.

recording costs; the group had recorded 469 songs while at Motown, of which only 174 had been released, and Gordy felt the others didn't meet the label's quality control standards. Joe Jackson still had to pay for them.

When the case finally came to court, Gordy was granted $600,000 in damages, plus a fee against the songs that could have been recorded in the ten-month period between Joe Jackson's announcement of the group's departure and the official expiry date of their contract. In addition, they would not earn any royalties on future issues of their Motown hits, and they would also need to surrender royalties on recordings made until December 1, 1979.[10] However, they *would* earn on releases of unreleased material and "best of" packages. The cost of freedom in all was somewhere in the region of two million dollars.

A CHILD NO MORE

Michael Jackson was by now sixteen, going on seventeen. He was growing up. Not since the days of Shirley Temple or Jackie Coogan had an adolescence been so closely scrutinized by the mass media. It was true that he looked awkward in some footage, but here was a young beautiful man, standing on the verge of so many possibilities. And, importantly, he would be granted a concurrent solo contract, just as he had with Motown. It was all a question of when he should make his first solo recording.

Michael Jackson was drinking in all that was around him; as he had been looked on so fondly by all his peers over the years, they were, of course, delighted to allow their teenage friend to sit and watch just what they were up to as they sculpted their own cultural legacy. "So Stevie Wonder used to literally let me sit like a fly on the wall. I got to see *Songs in the Key of Life* get made, some of the most golden things. I would sit with Marvin Gaye and just . . . and these would be the people who would just come over to our house and hang out and play basketball with my brothers on the weekend. We always had these people around. So when you really can see the science, the anatomy and the structure of how it all works, it's just so wonderful."[11] Given that Berry Gordy had known him as "Little Spongy," there was an incredible amount now around to absorb. And, boy, was Jackson absorbing it. Nothing would go to waste.

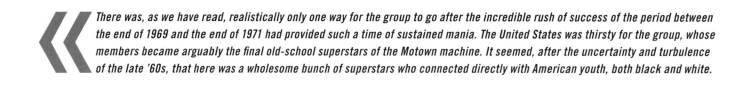

There was, as we have read, realistically only one way for the group to go after the incredible rush of success of the period between the end of 1969 and the end of 1971 had provided such a time of sustained mania. The United States was thirsty for the group, whose members became arguably the final old-school superstars of the Motown machine. It seemed, after the uncertainty and turbulence of the late '60s, that here was a wholesome bunch of superstars who connected directly with American youth, both black and white.

CHAPTER 14

ONE LONG SLEEPLESS NIGHT

JACKSONMANIA

"He not only studied me, but he studied James Brown, Jackie Wilson, Marcel Marceau. Fred Astaire . . . Walt Disney."

—BERRY GORDY, 1995[1]

MOVING ON

With their Steeltown single and their persistent fixture on the Chicago talent-contest circuit, people soon began to talk about this family group from Gary, Indiana. Gladys Knight was the first to mention the Jacksons to Berry Gordy after they supported her and the Pips in the Midwest and at the Apollo. But the outfit that would have the most profound effect on the brothers was Bobby Taylor and the Vancouvers. In July 1968, the Jackson 5 opened for them at Chicago's High Chaparral Club and the Regal Theater. Taylor was something of a journeyman with the most distinctive voice; importantly for the times, the Vancouvers were a mixed-race outfit. Although many backroom players in soul had been white, few had openly mixed-race outfits, aside from Booker T. before and Sly and the Family Stone soon after.

Bobby Taylor wanted to bring the Jacksons to Motown. They got the call to audition for the label at Hitsville USA in Detroit on July 23, 1968, in front of Motown executives Suzanne de Passe and Ralph Seltzer. (Much to the chagrin of Joe Jackson, Berry Gordy was away on business in Los Angeles.)

Motown, the sound of Young America, was in something of a state of flux by mid-1968, with its key writing and production team, Holland-Dozier-Holland, having departed the label over unpaid royalties and the shifting mores

OPPOSITE: *The LIFE cover of the Jackson 5 at home at Hayvenhurst, September 24, 1971.*

of the audience it had helped shape looking for something a little deeper than a simple pop song. With civil unrest on the streets due to racial inequality and music looking to weightier concepts, the label, for the first time in a decade, was made to reflect on its direction. A classic boy band could be just the ticket to offer something simpler and more direct to the marketplace.

Gordy saw the tape in L.A. and realized the explosive potential of the group's lead vocalist. Although he was initially unsure, he was, quite rightly, transfixed when he studied Michael, a tiny ball of energy, alive in the middle of the brothers. "He knew what he wanted. And from nine years old, he was a thinker. And I called him 'little spongy,' because he was a sponge and learned from everybody."[2]

The Jackson brothers were signed to Motown and put into development. The group played Gordy's Christmas party in 1968, creating a stir among their soon-to-be peers. Bobby Taylor took the brothers under his wing and nurtured their talent, recording soulful covers in line with their stage performances; this material would form the backbone of what was to become their debut album.

But soon Gordy would realize the group's potential and ask the family to relocate— lock, stock, and barrel—to Los Angeles, to be supervised by him and his number two, Suzanne de Passe. Motown executive vice-president Barney Ales was to note that de Passe "had taken them over. She dressed them, made them up, thought of Diana 'discovering' them, which was a great idea."[3]

It was indeed a shrewd idea to have the biggest star on the label introduce the Jackson

OPPOSITE: *Gladys Knight and the Pips performing on the* Ed Sullivan Show, *February 1968. Knight would be the first artist to recommend that Berry Gordy investigate the Jackson brothers.* **ABOVE:** *Berry Gordy at home in the 1960s, looking at all the countries where Motown had hits.*

5 to the wider world. Legend has it that Ross "discovered" the group when she saw them perform in Gary on September 27, 1968, when they opened a benefit show at Gilroy Stadium, with Bobby Taylor and Gladys Knight on the bill. In reality, she was nowhere near the show.[4] But what Ross certainly did do was nurture the group. After they agreed to Gordy's request to relocate to Los Angeles, some of the brothers (including Michael) stayed with Ross and others with Gordy before finding rented accommodation. "She was so wonderful," Jackson writes in *Moonwalk*.

"Mothering us and making us feel right at home."[5]

Gordy secured them the hottest ticket in town: supporting the Supremes on their final shows with Diana Ross. The appearance on the *Miss Black America* pageant in 1969 truly showed their limitless potential. Singing the Isley Brothers' "It's Your Thing," which at that moment was the coolest record known to mankind, they showed that they could emulate the best of them.

"I WANT YOU BACK"

The Jackson 5's debut single for Motown was an infectious ball of energy called "I Want You Back," a joyous fizz that sounded exactly like the group looked. Written by the Corporation™, it was as if the Jackson 5 had some fine, faceless factory behind them creating nuggets of solid gold, which was exactly what Gordy wanted.

In reality, the Corporation™ was Freddie Perren, Alphonzo Mizell, Deke Richards, and Gordy himself. The track had begun life as a song written for Gladys Knight called "I Want to Be Free" by Perren, Mizell, and Richards. When the writers and producers heard that the Bobby Taylor sessions were not full of hits for the young Jacksons, Gordy got involved with the track, allegedly asking his staff to "give the song a Frankie Lymon treatment."[6] From that moment on, the legend was born. Richards worked around the clock with the boys for the next three weeks, getting their vocal interplay correct and teaching Michael, as the group's lead vocalist, to enunciate properly.

The Jackson 5's musical contributions to the record were nonexistent; David T. Walker and Louie Shelton took the lead lines and future

Crusader Wilton Felder replaced Jermaine on bass. Gene Pello played drums and Sandra Crouch added tambourine. The greatest coup of the record, however, was keeping the vocal interplay between the brothers.

Released in October 1969, with a Taylor-produced soulful cover of Smokey Robinson's "Who's Loving You" on its flip, "I Want You Back" took its time to climb to the US No. 1 spot, but slowly and surely, like the snowball down the hill, it gathered fans and followers that propelled it further up the charts.

In December 1969, the brothers appeared on the ultimate American institution, *The Ed Sullivan Show*. Sullivan, all angles and bumps, looked out at his audience with the considerable unease he had made his trademark, and said, "That's really a ten strike; the little fellow in front is incredible." And it was absolutely true: the little fellow out in front was exactly that.

On January 31, 1970, one month after the new decade had gotten underway, "I Want You Back" stood brazenly atop the US singles charts. *Rolling Stone* captured it perfectly when it said, "The record explodes off the turntable."[7]

DIANA ROSS PRESENTS THE JACKSON 5

"I Want You Back" was the only single taken from the group's debut album. The album, *Diana Ross Presents the Jackson 5*, was released in December 1969, and the lead single shouted clearly the direction in which they were to go. Although the majority of the album is comprised of Bobby Taylor–produced covers, it was the two Corporation™ tracks that were to define the sound

The endless hours of home practice and an apprenticeship in the clubs meant that when the group hit TV screens in 1969, they were already seasoned performers.

(the other being "Nobody"). The sleeve contains a lengthy essay, attributed to Diana Ross, about how she discovered the group. There is a mention of Bobby Taylor, credited as "the first professional to work with the guys." "They've got great talent, and above all, they are honest," Ross writes. The inner bags were full of adverts for J5 merchandise and opportunities to join their fan club. Already. The album sold over half a million copies and went to No. 5 on *Billboard*. There was very clearly an appetite for this youthful breath of fresh air.

Within months, there was a clamor for more music. And fortunately, with the production line setup, more could follow quickly. The lead single from their second album was waiting in the wings: released at the end of February, "ABC" was almost identical in sound to "I Want You Back." By the end of April, just before the release of their album of the same name, "ABC" knocked

LEFT: *The Jackson 5 with their mentor, Diana Ross. Her patronage was key in Gordy's launch plans for the group.*
ABOVE: *The debut album is packed full of joie de vivre.*

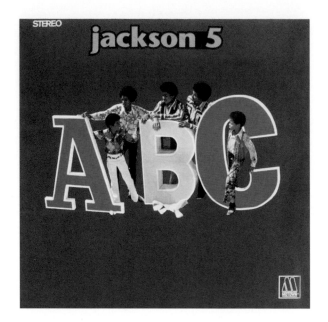

the Beatles' "Let It Be" off the top spot in the United States. This was huge news from a group that had been unheard of less than a year before.

Released at the start of May, its parent album, *ABC*, had one huge homogenized sound to it; the Corporation™ is all over it. As I was later to write, "Perhaps by their very nature, the best Jackson 5 album will forever be one of the endless hits collections to bear their name. That said, *ABC* is a fine work that shows maturity beyond their years. In many ways, this is the template for every boy band long-player since—just enough soul, just enough raunch, lashings of pathos, all bound together with an elegant sufficiency of feel-good sentiment . . . overall *ABC* is beautiful bubblegum soul. Listen to it instead of watching the next documentary about him and a chimp on the telly."[8]

The second single from the album, "The Love You Save," gave the group a third number one single—and their second dethroning of the Beatles, removing "The Long and Winding Road" from the top spot. The last of the group's copycat singles, "The Love You Save" is a joyous sound, an ebullient warning for a girl not to go too fast.

THIRD ALBUM

It is the group's third album (helpfully called *Third Album*), released in September 1970, that contains arguably the most significant song of the Jackson 5's career. Written by Willie Hutch, Berry Gordy, Bob West Jr., and Hal Davis, "I'll Be There" was their first grown up song. " 'I'll Be There' was our real breakthrough song," Jackson was to say. "It was the one that said, 'We're here to stay.' It was No. 1 for five weeks, which is very unusual . . . we were feeling part of Motown's history as well as its future."[9]

It was a stunning, history-making record, the lightest of touches that shows the group's softer side—a bold move after the onslaught of bubblegum on the first releases. Jermaine's vocal in the bridge before handing back to Michael is one of the most powerful moments in popular music. Michael's reference to "Reach Out, I'll Be There" came at Gordy's suggestion; adding "honey" to the end, he creates a truly unique moment. The song became Motown's biggest-selling single in the United States until 1981. Berry Gordy would tell everyone that he felt that Michael Jackson had been here before,

as he had the soulful quality of someone much older than he was. His delivery on this record seems to underline this. The *Third Album* itself would be the group's biggest seller, selling around six million copies worldwide. It showed the group maturing, with solos being shared by band members. It also features the follow-up to "I'll Be There"—"Mama's Pearl"—which took the group back to their early sound. A straight Corporation™ confection, it was to reach No. 2 in early 1971.

JACKSONMANIA

A fourteen-date tour ran intermittently through 1970; a one-off show at the Spectrum in Philadelphia in May was followed by two further shows in Daly City and Inglewood in June, before a run of shows began in October. It was here that Jacksonmania was truly witnessed.

By the end of 1970, the Jackson 5's popularity was such that they had two of the highest accolades that could be bestowed on any group—it was announced that they were to get their own cartoon series, while there was another group plainly emulating their style.

The cartoon show, *The Jackson 5ive*, premiered on September 11, 1971. In total, twenty-three episodes of the thirty-minute series were made by Rankin/Bass, in conjunction with Motown Productions. As with the Beatles' cartoon series from the mid-'60s and 1968's *Yellow Submarine*, voice actors were to play the brothers, yet the Jacksons contributed to the series' opening sequence by transforming into their cartoon characters, as well as recording a medley of their hits for the show's titles.

OPPOSITE TOP: *ABC was almost an identical version of the first album, and had a rushed release to capitalize on their first wave of success.* OPPOSITE BOTTOM: *The Third Album contains "I'll Be There," a significant change in musical direction for the group.* ABOVE: *The Christmas Album: for many, the holiday season is not complete without young Michael squealing with joy at the thought of Santa Claus comin' to town.*

In late 1970, the Jackson 5 saw their clearest rivals top the charts. The Osmond family, a troupe of Mormon brothers from Utah, had had their image revamped by MGM label boss Mike Curb. In second-youngest brother Donny, they had their own heartthrob. "One Bad Apple," which could be called an "affectionate homage" to "I Want You Back," was written by George Jackson, and had been offered to Gordy for the Jackson 5. Produced by Rick Hall, it became a smash. The Jackson 5 had invented bubblegum soul. "Imitation is the sincerest form of flattery," Motown vice-president Ewart Abner said. "We here at Motown are not mad at anybody. We wish them luck, while we go on doing our thing and they go on doing our thing."[10]

To finish their triumphant 1970, the mainly non-Christmas-believing Jehovah's Witness Jackson 5 released their one foray into the festive market with their *Christmas Album*. It has gone on to be a perennial seller, and for many the holiday season is not complete without young Michael squealing with joy at the thought of Santa Claus coming to town.

MAYBE TOMORROW

The year 1971 was all about coming to terms with and living with their fame. At last, after a year of renting in Los Angeles, the Jacksons found an established home at the Hayvenhurst estate, where the whole family would live. At the end of January, the family returned for a series of concerts in Gary—their first time there since leaving for California. Playing for Mayor Richard Hatcher's re-election campaign, they receive the keys to the city; their street was renamed "Jackson 5 Boulevard" for the occasion. The event was filmed and formed the basis of a television special later in the year.

Released in April 1971, *Maybe Tomorrow*, the fifth album by the Jackson 5, has the brothers looking pensive on the sleeve, aside from a smiling Michael. They all looked thoroughly weary from the twelve months of fame. Five albums and seven singles on, they had more than proved themselves;

ABOVE: *Jackson at the piano, Los Angeles, 1971.* OPPOSITE: *Biker gang: the Jacksons in the backyard for their LIFE feature, September 1971.*

it was also clear that ballads could be the way forward, and so the lead track from the album was the sensual "Never Can Say Goodbye." It was written by actor Clifton Davis, initially for the Supremes, before Gordy diverted the song to the brothers. It reached No. 2 again in the United States.

It was hard to avoid the Jackson 5. They featured prominently in Diana Ross' prestigious *Diana!* ABC TV special, broadcast on April 18, 1971, alongside fellow guests Danny Thomas and Bill Cosby. It was on this show that Jackson also made his solo debut, singing a humorously amended version of Frank Sinatra's "It Was a Very Good Year." There was a fabulous section on the show where the group sings Traffic's "Feelin' Alright" and Ross herself comes on; as Jackson clings to the center stage, Ross forcibly ejects him. His face is a picture, a surly thirteen-year-old thrown from the spotlight. He may have been a star, but no one takes Ms. Ross' place.

With a forty-date US tour running through the summer, it didn't seem to matter that, when released as a single, the title track of *Maybe Tomorrow* only reached No. 20 in the United States. It was the first of their singles not to make the Top 5. The cartoon series started in September, and magazines like *Life*, *Rolling Stone*, and *Ebony* all featured the group as cover stars. Their concert at Madison Square Garden had to be repeatedly stopped due to crowd surges.

In September, ABC broadcast the hugely ambitious television extravaganza *Goin' Back to Indiana*, filmed in Gary back in January. It perfectly sold their story back to an eager America, with guest appearances from Bill Cosby, Tommy Smothers, Diana Ross, and Bobby Darin. Centered around their homecoming concerts, it featured the group in skits between songs. The accompanying album captured not only this exuberance but also quite how accomplished they had become as players and performers.

GREATEST HITS

Released just after Christmas in December 1971, *Greatest Hits* sweetly and succinctly closed off the high-water mark era of the Jackson 5. Its cover is a picture of them in a gilt-edged frame, making them look like they had been captured by an old master. If they never had recorded another note, these thirty-seven minutes would have been their lasting statement for history: nine hits and much-loved album tracks, plus the previously unreleased "Sugar Daddy," recorded earlier that year. The album was to sell over five million copies worldwide. Its triumphal air seemed to suggest that things might never be as great as this ever again.

The impact of the Jackson 5 was absolutely enormous. The group—young, gifted, and black—spoke to the youth of America in a way that some of Motown's grandees no longer did. Future sensation Terence Trent D'Arby, interviewed in 1993, spoke for millions. "I kept thinking, even as a child, that there was something else, besides gospel, to sing, and then I heard the Jackson 5 and it was like a whole new world opening for me. It was like I had found my own world."[11]

OPPOSITE: *A still from the* Goin' Back to Indiana *TV special, 1971.*

It all rewinds back to the very beginning, before the lucky break of being signed to Motown, to the town of Gary, Indiana, where Joe and Katherine Jackson brought up their sizeable family. Joe Jackson was a steel worker and amateur musician who, with his wife Katherine, herself a singer, encouraged their nine children to perform. By the start of 1968, less than ten years after he was born, Michael Jackson could be heard as the lead vocalist on the group's debut 45.

CHAPTER 15

GOT TO BE THERE

GARY, INDIANA

"My father would rehearse with a belt in his hand. You couldn't mess up.
My father was a genius when it comes to the way he taught us, staging, how to work
an audience, anticipating what to do next, or never let the audience know if you
are suffering, or if something's going wrong. He was amazing like that."

—MICHAEL JACKSON, 2007[1]

Michael Jackson was hardly born into a showbusiness family. By the time he had arrived in 1958, his mother, Katherine, and father, Joe, had six older children, and were both working all hours in order to provide food and shelter for their offspring. Both loved music and were keen to encourage a similar passion in their children.

Joseph Walter Jackson was born on July 26, 1928, in Fountain Hill, Arkansas. The eldest of five children, his parents split up when he was twelve; he moved to East Chicago with his mother and two brothers, before spending time with his father in Oakland, California. At the age of eighteen, Joe Jackson returned to East Chicago and took a job at the Inland Steel Company. Situated on the Indiana Harbor Ship Canal, Inland Steel specialized in cold-rolled sheet and strip steel for car production. Jackson would bring in the iron ore and coal from Lake Michigan to the factory. He also wanted to be a boxer, and trained through the Golden Gloves Association of America. He was also married, but was divorced soon after meeting Katherine Scruse at a local party.

Scruse was born in Clayton, Alabama on May 4, 1930. After suffering from polio as a child, she became shy and introverted, and walked with a limp. Along with her sister, Hattie, she harbored dreams of singing and dancing. She and Jackson were immediately attracted to each other, and after his separation from his first wife became official, the pair began dating. The two were married at Crown Point, Indiana, on November 5, 1949. Katherine's parents had

OPPOSITE: *One of the first shots of the brothers—little did they know what the next few years would have in store for them.*

Gary Works: the US Steel plant that once dominated the city's economy.

also divorced, so with two parental splits and this being Joseph's second marriage, Katherine was determined that the two would stay together through thick and thin. Both loved music. And importantly, each other.

The young couple settled into Gary in Lake County, Indiana, a satellite town twenty-five miles from the center of Chicago, in a two-bedroomed house at—coincidentally—2300 Jackson Street. The children soon began arriving. Maureen (Rebbie) was born on May 29, 1950, and Joseph realized he had to put his boxing aspirations

behind him; a crane worker he would remain—for the time being. His daily shift at Inland Steel from 4 p.m. to midnight meant he earned enough to support a young wife and daughter.

Further children arrived: Sigmund Esco (Jackie) on May 4, 1951; Tariano Adaryl (Tito) on October 15, 1953; Jermaine LaJuane on December 11, 1954; LaToya Yvonne on May 29, 1956; twins Marlon David and Brandon (who sadly died at childbirth) on March 12, 1957; Michael Joseph on August 29, 1958; Steven Randall on October 29, 1961; and, finally, their youngest, Janet Damita Jo, on May 15, 1966.

THE FALCONS AND THE JACKSON BROTHERS

Money, as one can imagine, was scarce. Katherine took a part-time job at the local Sears, and Joe Jackson became part of an R&B group, the Falcons, with his brother, Luther. The Falcons brought in some extra income as they worked the bars and clubs of greater Chicago. They would rehearse at 2300 Jackson Street, and although Michael Jackson would have been too young to recall them, the band would make a great impression on his elder brothers. The Falcons ultimately came to nothing, and Jackson began working at American Foundries to supplement his Inland Steel income.

It was in 1963 that Joe Jackson began to realize the musical potential of his children. Jackie (vocals), Jermaine (guitar), and Tito (guitar) began to rehearse together as a band; soon young Marlon and Michael would join them, principally on percussion. He made them practice, before and after school. As biographer J. Randy Taraborrelli notes, "Though the Jacksons' music may have brought them closer together as a family unit, it also served to further alienate them from everyone else in their neighborhood."[2] This alienation was in part due to the fact that Katherine Jackson became a Jehovah's Witness in 1963; it remains her faith to this day, and all of her children would follow her into it. With their highly individual proselytizing brand of Christianity, the religion marked the family out as different.

WITH A CHILD'S HEART

There is little doubting how hard Joe Jackson worked for his family. There is also little doubt, as chronicled extensively elsewhere, that he was not afraid to use old-fashioned methods of discipline to bring his children into line. And, being such a sensitive soul, Michael Jackson was terrorized by his father from the off. Unlike his other siblings, he frequently fought back, which invariably landed him in much, much greater trouble.

Katherine did not approve of her husband's actions, and would be on hand to dispense love and understanding to her son. As Nelson George writes in one of the very first biographies of Jackson, "The firm hand of father Joseph and the caressing words of Katherine instilled Michael and his three sisters and five brothers with values that run deeper than the surface thrills of pop music."[3] There was also little doubt that Michael had skills way beyond those of the rest of his family; he was, allegedly, dancing in time at eighteen months old, and by the age of four he was clearly mimicking elder brother Jermaine's vocal style.

In 1963, at the age of five, Jackson began school at Garnett Elementary, two blocks away from his home. It was here that he sang in a concert a version of Rodgers and Hammerstein's "Climb Ev'ry Mountain," a capella. Katherine, Joe, and his father Sam attended. There was not a dry eye in the house. It was performances like this, and the five-year-old's already-natural performance confidence, that made Jackie, the eldest of the group, decide that even, at this young age, Michael should be the group's lead singer. Although Jermaine, who had been singing to that point, was clearly somewhat perplexed, he could already appreciate Michael's ability for the limelight, and for impersonations, and his most remarkably pure singing voice. Jackson was like a sponge, "watching everything and trying to learn all I could."[4]

With family friend Johnny Porter Jackson (no relation, although he was billed for years as cousin) on drums, Ronnie Rancifer on keyboards, Tito on guitar, and Jermaine on bass, the Jackson Brothers became a group. Not that the name was to last long: in conversation with Evelyn Leahy, who had organized a contest in a shopping mall in Gary, she told Joe that the name the Jackson Brothers sounded old-fashioned, and he should call them simply "the Jackson Five."

JACKSONS GET LUCKY

The talent contest circuit was proving successful for the Jacksons as a way of honing their craft. They started winning contents when Michael was six, and before long they had set the pattern for their performances, right down to the order they would stand in onstage: Jermaine stage left, with Michael to his side, then Jackie and Marlon, with Tito stage right with his guitar. Their professionalism served them well. "While other groups we'd meet would fight among themselves and quit," Jackson later wrote, "we were becoming more polished and experienced."[5] Sometimes the group would drive over 200 miles in a night, just to gain more experience for a contest, honing their fledgling act into just two songs. A particular showstopper of Michael's was

ABOVE: *The Martin Luther King Academy, Gary, Indiana: until 1970, this was Garnett Elementary School, where Michael and his brothers attended.* OPPOSITE: *With Johnny Porter Jackson on drums, this shot from around 1966 features a pensive Michael.*

One of the important venues where the group learned their craft: the Apollo Theater, Harlem, New York City, in the mid-60s.

to take off his shoes and dance barefooted in the middle eight of Robert Parker's "Barefootin'."

A turning point came when the group won the citywide talent contest at Roosevelt High School on 730 W. 25th Avenue in 1966, after performing a version of "My Girl." Michael would later recall that the audience was on its feet from the opening notes of the song; afterward, "it was a wonderful feeling for all of us to pass that trophy, our biggest yet, back and forth between us." On the way home, Joe Jackson told them, "When you do it like you did tonight, they can't not give it to you."[6] They were now the Gary City Champions, and from there they could break into the Chicago circuit.

Later in 1966, they won the annual talent search at Gilroy Stadium. This led to a residency at Mr. Lucky's, a nightclub on the corner of East 11th Avenue and Grant Street in Gary, earning eight dollars a night for five sets up to seven days a week. The group would play in between comedians, singers, and strippers. It was here the young Michael would regularly crawl under tables and look up the skirts of the female audience members, much to the cheers of encouragement of the crowd. Suffice it to say, while his brothers and father felt this "all part of the act," mother Katherine knew nothing of what her eight-year-old son was up to.

It was around this time that Joe Jackson sent a demo tape of the group to Berry Gordy, the founder of Motown Records. It was later returned without an offer. The group would spend time playing on the fabled chitlin' circuit, performing at 2,000-seater venues in places such as Cleveland and Baltimore. Jackson would bring the children home at around five in the morning; they would sleep briefly and then go off to school. In August 1967, the group played the Apollo Theater in Harlem, very much the principal venue of R&B. Jackson slavishly noted all of the performers' moves around him as he stood in the wings.

STEELTOWN AND "BIG BOY"

Local record producer Gordon Keith came to see the Jackson Five at a talent show at Beckman Junior High in Gary. Keith was an enthusiastic amateur: a millworker by day and a singer and small-singles record-company boss by night.

Impressed by what he saw, he immediately signed the band to his label, Steeltown, on a deal that saw them receive three cents per record sold, to be split between the five brothers and drummer Johnny Jackson. The group, who played the majority of the instruments on the sessions, recorded at Keith's home studio at West 10th Avenue and Taney Street on the weekend.

On January 30, 1968—the day that North Vietnam launched the decisive Tet Offensive in the Vietnam War—Michael Jackson made his debut on vinyl. Billed to the Jackson Five, "Big Boy," written by local musician Eddie Silvers, was a classic growing-up ballad in the style that Frankie Lymon had perfected. "Of course, to get the full picture, you have to imagine a skinny nine-year-old singing this song," Jackson later noted. "I was far too young to grasp the real meanings of most of the words in these songs."[7]

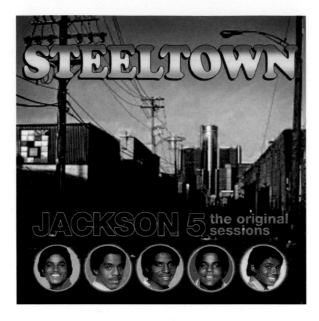

Initially distributed by the band at their concerts, the single became enough of a local hit to be picked up for distribution by Atco, allegedly at the request of Jerry Wexler, and around 10,000 copies were pressed. What it did ensure was that the bigger venues in Chicago became truly receptive to the group, and soon they would be supporting bigger stars. In 1970, after the band had broken through, Keith dusted down the next best track, "We Don't Have to Be Over 21 (to Fall in Love)," backed it with "Jam Session," and released it as a single.

The complete Steeltown sessions have emerged on a variety of releases across the years, starting in the CD age with *The Jackson 5 and Johnny: Beginning Years 1967–1968*. To hear all the work they recorded for Gordon Keith is endearing, as the collection is full of the roughest jams they made, and, aside from Jackson's already striking vocal style (albeit in all its youthful unfinished-ness), they sound just like any other teenage garage band: basic, with faltering, occasionally tuneless playing, yet undeniably revealing a spark.

On the full recordings, Jackson is caught as just what he was, a nine-year-old happily not believing his luck and playing up somewhat for the microphone. "Boys and girls, we are the Jackson 5, and we are happy to entertain on this show," he says. "We hope you like our songs. The first song will be the introduction. Let it roll!" Another brother pipes up, "*The introduction is not a song*." Featuring covers of "A Change Is Gonna Come," "My Girl," and "Under the Boardwalk," the complete recordings are a wonderful selection of juvenilia; a starting point demonstrating the raw sound that others were soon to fall in love with.

And, like so many hundreds of thousands of other teenage groups, this is where it could have all ended, puttering out with a first flush of success, some local press clippings in a scrapbook, a dusty groove in a sleeve, high on a shelf. But those who saw this strange, ahead-of-the-curve ten-year-old knew that there was a huge future ahead for him and his brothers.

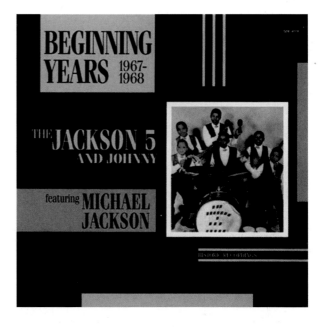

TOP AND ABOVE: *The group's first recordings for Steeltown have been repackaged in a variety of configurations across the years; here are two of them.* **OPPOSITE:** *Just before signing to Motown, this photo highlights the group's increasing professionalism.*

"I will allways love You"
The Jackson Five

And so, as we end at the beginning, we return to the end. We all know what happened to that beautiful bundle of hope and joy from Indiana, whose remarkable exuberance and natural talent was able to captivate the world in a manner that few artists have ever attempted. And, of course, with this being the story of Michael Jackson, there continues to be spectacle and surprise long after he has left the planet himself.

LOVE NEVER FELT SO GOOD

"In my opinion, it's ignorance. It's usually not based on fact. It's based on, you know, myth. The guy who you don't get to see. Every neighborhood has the guy who you don't see, so you gossip about him. You see those stories about him, there's the myth that he did this or he did that. People are crazy! I'm just about wanting to do wonderful music."

— MICHAEL JACKSON, 2007[1]

"It's time to look on in awe as Jackson's memory—and the legendary fervency of his fans—is ruthlessly exploited till the pips squeak."

— ANDREW PULVER, THE *GUARDIAN*, 2009[2]

In the last week of October 2009, Michael Jackson did something that arguably would not have happened at this point in his life: he embarked upon a world tour. The film of the rehearsals and months leading up to the shows-that-never-were was released as *Michael Jackson's This Is It*.

The piecing-together of the film generated $200 million—a huge amount considering the footage was only to be used sparingly at best in a full concert documentary. *Michael Jackson's This Is It* was released in eight thousand theaters worldwide, with an additional three thousand in the United States—a huge amount for what was fundamentally a rock documentary, specialist at best. As Andrew Pulver wrote in the *Guardian*, "*This Is It* is a testament of a kind, and one that is no disgrace to his memory."[3]

Although the *This Is It* tour never got off the ground, revenue from tickets retained by fans as souvenirs and not refunded brought in about $6.5 million, with merchandise raking in a further $5 million, although

OPPOSITE: *Cirque du Soleil's* Michael Jackson: The Immortal World Tour *in Madrid, December 2012.*

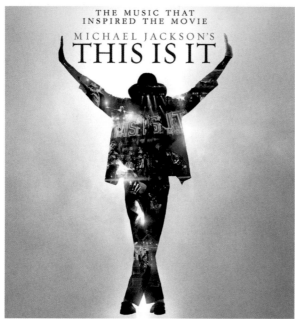

concert promoter AEG would take a cut of these profits.

In November 2009, the album *This Is It* returned Jackson to the top of the US charts for the first time since *Invincible* in 2001. The album was a classic repackage: "*The Music That Inspired the Motion Picture*." It was another thirteen Jackson/Jacksons classics, served in a double-edition with four demos. The real draw was the *de facto* theme song, "This Is It," which was released as a radio track; co-written with

Paul Anka, it had overdubbed backing vocals by Michael's brothers Tito, Jermaine, Marlon, and Jackie. It sounds not unlike an outtake from a Jacksons album, and provides a rather lovely coda to the project.

In March 2010, the Jackson estate and Sony launched into a seven-year deal that was estimated to be worth around $250 million; a press release proclaimed proudly, "We and Sony feel that the future for Michael Jackson is unlimited. If you look at Elvis and the Beatles, and how their brands are thriving, they only hint at what the future holds for Michael."[4]

Long-serving engineer Bruce Swedien said at the time of Jackson's death, "I'm going to be messing around with Michael's stuff. I've gone back to most of the old stuff . . . I have been involved with some of the new material, but I have no idea of what they are intending to do. There is some wonderful stuff there."

The "wonderful stuff" to date has made it onto two releases, 2010's *Michael*, which features material recorded in the period after 2001, and the much more satisfying *Xscape*, which was helmed by L.A. Reid. This release features material from 1983–1999; its lead single, "Love Never Felt So Good," put Jackson back in the US and UK Top 10. Given the additional repackages, there is a strong feeling that this element of Jackson's legacy will run and run.

The inquest into Michael Jackson's death decreed, on February 8, 2010, that Propofol dosage and negligence killed the pop legend. In a court case in 2011, Conrad Murray was found guilty of negligence. After eight hours of jury deliberation, he was sentenced to four years in prison.

Believing that AEG Live had failed to effectively protect the singer while he was under

Murray's care, the Jackson family decided to take legal action against the company. Katherine Jackson, alongside Blanket, Michael Jr. and Paris, officially filed a wrongful death lawsuit against AEG, and the trial began in April 2013. In October that year, the court ruled against the family. It was stated that the entertainment giant had "hired Murray at the request of Jackson and had no knowledge of the star's drug dependency."[5]

FROM MOTOWN TO OFF THE WALL

In 2012, acclaimed film director Spike Lee made the first of two in-depth profiles of Jackson's career, *Bad 25*. With fifty interviewees and a running time of 130 minutes, few stones are left unturned; to update the story, and keep Jackson current, Justin Bieber is one of the talking heads among fans such as Mariah Carey and Kanye West. Members of the studio team are on hand, including the permanently engaging engineer Bruce Swedien and scene-stealer Greg Phillinganes, the seasoned keyboard player. Shalamar body popper Jeffery Daniel appears frequently, talking about the choreography for the "Bad" and "Smooth Criminal" videos. There is

also an interesting section about how Jackson's dancing had been influenced by *Soul Train*, the program on which Daniel had made his name.

It's a celebratory piece, of course, and, made in tandem with the estate, is relatively unquestioning. Even so, Lee, who worked with Jackson on his 1996 video "They Don't Care About Us," manages to successfully put together an exhaustive, entertaining remembrance of the time.

Lee's remarkable second documentary, *Michael Jackson's Journey from Motown to Off the Wall*, again captures the Jackson everyone

OPPOSITE TOP: Michael: *The first posthumous release of previously unreleased material.* OPPOSITE BOTTOM: This Is It *returned Jackson to the top of the US charts.* TOP: Xscape, *the second posthumous album of previously unreleased material, demonstrates just how Jackson's musical legacy should be dealt with properly.* ABOVE: *Conrad Murray reacts to his guilty verdict, Los Angeles Superior Court, November 2011.*

27, 2016, Jones filed a lawsuit against the Jackson estate for unpaid royalties on the music he produced that has subsequently been used in posthumous recordings and releases.

ONE

In 2015, Michael Jackson was listed by *Forbes* magazine for the sixth successive year as being the highest-earning deceased celebrity, having earned, by the end of that year, $115 million. He beat his one-time father-in-law, Elvis Presley, into second place, with Presley having grossed a mere $55 million. As *Forbes* explained in its countdown, "The King of Pop has earned triple-digit millions every full year since his death in 2009. The prime drivers of his afterlife fortune: permanent Vegas Cirque du Soleil show *Michael Jackson One*, the Mijac Music catalogue, recorded music sales, and half of the Sony/ATV publishing empire."[6]

One part of that was to change forever: on March 14, 2016, it was announced that Sony was to buy out Jackson's share of ATV publishing for a reported sum of $750 million. The ever-loyal John Branca was still overseeing the best deals for his long-serving client. He and John McClain issued a statement that said, "This transaction further allows us to continue our efforts of maximizing the value of Michael's Estate for the benefit of his children. It also further validates Michael's foresight and genius in investing in music publishing. His ATV catalogue, purchased in 1985 for a net acquisition cost of $41.5 million, was the cornerstone of the joint venture and, as evidenced by the value of this transaction, is considered one of the smartest investments in music history." The deal, which should be finalized in 2017,

wanted to remember: young, vibrant, vital, growing up—the nation's teenager. Released as a double-pack with the CD, the package came complete—unbelievably—with a stick of chalk, to allow fans to "create your own art on the specially treated brick wall on the inside of the package." Fans were encouraged to post their creations on the Michael Jackson social media pages.

Off the Wall's successor, *Thriller*, is rarely out of the news. In 2016, it was certified as thirty-two times platinum in America alone. Quincy Jones posted this message to Instagram: "Extremely proud of all the hard work that went into *Thriller*, which just became the first album in RIAA's 63-year history to become 30x multi-platinum in the United States. We never expected it to sell 30 million copies in America, let alone, over 100 million copies worldwide—but I'm glad some of you liked it! Miss you Smelly, but I bet you're up there celebrating by teaching everyone the 'Thriller' dance!"

And yet, as if to show the ongoing complexities of Jackson's dealings, on February

still allows the family to control Mijac music, which owns all of the Michael Jackson copyrights, and also a 10 percent stake in EMI Publishing.

"WAS I LUCKY OR WHAT?"

Of all the many things written about Jackson, one of the most touching came from his long-term engineer Bruce Swedien. "Michael Jackson was the best. Not just as a vocalist but as a musician. He took it to the sky. He could play piano a little but he wasn't that kind of a musician. Michael's instrument was his voice and his ideas. Quincy's instrument, and mine, I guess, was the studio. It was such a great thing working with Michael; we just kept pushing the musical boundaries. Was I lucky or what?"[/]

Now Jackson shines on, unassailable in his position as the King of Pop. As memories fade and books are balanced, everyone remembers the time of Michael Jackson as the shining, strident super-in-the-making of the years between 1977 and 1987, bolstered by Spike Lee documentaries and the cult of nostalgia. What is interesting, however, is that, as Nelson George notes in his book *Thriller: The Musical Life of Michael Jackson*, younger people have no problem with the two Michael Jacksons: the black one and the white one. It is only those who grew up with him who find his persona change so difficult to grasp.

At the time of writing, Michael Jackson feels invincible in a way that he did not during the last half of his career. It is, one concludes, the old

OPPOSITE: *Bad 25's release coincided with Spike Lee's in-depth documentary about the album.* BELOW: *A sneak peak of Cirque du Soleil's* Michael Jackson: ONE, *Mandalay Bay, Las Vegas, May 2013.*

showbiz story: the tears of a clown—how can one man who brought to so much happiness spend his twilight in such abject misery? Now, simply, there is nothing but the pure, unalloyed pleasure of his tunes; there is a family growing up somewhere that tells his tales, and brothers and a devoted record label who curate his legacy. Everyone has grown old—except, of course, for Michael.

In his purest form, as time passes, Michael Jackson may be the single most important artist of the entire twentieth century. It's not just that he was the most commercially successful, but that he genuinely did seem to synthesize black and white music in a way that nobody else had done. The very fact that his entire being became an experiment almost for the fusion between the two makes it all the more striking. With all this time we have spent rewinding, Michael Jackson seemed to work only at one pace: fast-forward.

ABOVE: *Prince, Blanket, and Paris at the Michael Forever Tribute Concert, Cardiff, Wales, October 2011.* **LEFT:** *Bruce Swedien and Quincy Jones at the Pensado Awards, 2015.*

MICHAEL JACKSON SOLO ALBUM DISCOGRAPHY

GOT TO BE THERE (Motown, January 1972, No. 14 US / No. 37 UK)
Ain't No Sunshine / I Wanna Be Where You Are / Girl Don't Take Your Love from Me / In Our Small Way / Got to Be There / Rockin' Robin / Wings of My Love / Maria (You Were the Only One) / Love Is Here and Now You're Gone / You've Got a Friend

The first Michael Jackson album was released at the absolute zenith of the initial wave of the Jackson 5's popularity, and the title track built on the success that the group had enjoyed with "I'll Be There." With this album, produced by Hal Davis, the Corporation™, and Willie Hutch, Jackson established himself as the teenage friend you could go to with a problem; a shoulder to cry on. Despite the amount of balladry on the record, its joyous centerpiece, "Rockin' Robin," showed that Jackson had far from abandoned the dance floor. Most importantly, the album gave a resounding green light to Jackson's career outside of his group.

BEN (Motown, August 1972, No. 5 US / No. 17 UK)
Ben / Greatest Show on Earth / People Make the World Go Round / We've Got a Good Thing Going / Everybody's Somebody's Fool / My Girl / What Goes Around Comes Around / In Our Small Way / Shoo-Be-Do-Be-Doo-Da-Day / You Can Cry on My Shoulder

Jackson's most successful Motown solo album was propelled by the success of its Oscar-nominated title track, still possibly the only love song written about vermin to top the US charts. It is the apex of Jackson's period as the final true product of the Motown Hit Factory, recorded before his voice broke. There is an absolute zest to the material here, from the cover of "My Girl" to the joy of "The Greatest Show on Earth." Better still is the version of the Stylistics' "People Make the World Go Round." It remains a protest song, but with the lyrics adapted for a fourteen-year-old.

MUSIC & ME (Motown, April 1973, No. 92 US / – UK)
With a Child's Heart / Up Again / All the Things You Are / Happy / Too Young / Doggin' Around / Euphoria / Morning Glow / Johnny Raven / Music & Me

Music & Me is a transitional album for Jackson, who is pictured on the cover behind an oversized acoustic guitar, caught between child and adult. "With a Child's Heart," first sung by Stevie Wonder in 1966 (when he was a similar age to Jackson) opens the album in an assuredly mellow fashion, setting the tone for a sweet record that felt out-of-step with its time. "All the Things You Are," "Up Again," and "Happy (Love Theme from *Lady Sings the Blues*)" are all beautifully delivered; the title track is sweet; the only moment that truly thrills is age of Aquarius-soul of the Leon Ware–Jacqueline Hillard composition "Euphoria."

FOREVER, MICHAEL (Motown, January 1975, No. 101 US / – UK) We're Almost There / Take Me Back / One Day in Your Life / Cinderella Stay Awhile / We've Got Forever / Just a Little Bit of You / You Are There / Dapper-Dan / Dear Michael / I'll Come Home to You

Almost limping out and not even entering the US Top 100, *Forever, Michael* is an assured record; a snapshot of a maturing artist. Recorded in late 1974, the album features several affecting ballads, including lead single "We're Almost There." Feeling that this album was overlooked, Motown cashed in on the later success of *Off the Wall* by repackaging six of its tracks as the 1981 release *One Day in Your Life*, spurred on by the worldwide success of the track of the same name, the Sam Brown III–Renée Armand–penned standout from the album.

THRILLER (Epic, November 1982, No. 1 US / No. 1 UK) Wanna Be Startin' Somethin' / Baby Be Mine / The Girl Is Mine / Thriller / Beat It / Billie Jean / Human Nature / P.Y.T. (Pretty Young Thing) / The Lady in My Life

The most important album of the final quarter of the twentieth century, *Thriller* transcended being a mere record release in 1983 after Jackson appeared on US primetime TV performing "Billie Jean." From then on, this sleek confection had a life of its own; around the world, people fell in love with the sleek pop of "P.Y.T.," the tenderness of "Human Nature," and the raucous African-inspired funk of "Wanna Be Startin' Somethin'." And all of this is before the welding of heavy metal and dance on "Beat It." After John Landis directed the video for the title track, nearly a year after the album's release, *Thriller* became a global phenomenon.

OFF THE WALL (Epic, August 1979, No. 3 US / No. 3 UK) Don't Stop 'til You Get Enough / Rock with You / Working Day and Night / Get on the Floor / Off the Wall / Girlfriend / She's Out of My Life / I Can't Help It / It's the Falling in Love / Burn This Disco Out

One of the greatest records made by anyone—ever. Few records capture the upside of an era as does *Off the Wall*, which was inspired by Jackson's time living in New York during the making of *The Wiz*. Made with seasoned professionals (led by Quincy Jones) who placed Jackson at the center of their universe, *Off the Wall* opens on such a gloriously strong note (with "Don't Stop 'til You Get Enough") that the rest of the album could have all been filler and it would still have been loved. Fortunately, it most certainly isn't. Away from the floor, "She's Out of My Life" showed Jackson's maturity with a ballad. Just beautiful.

BAD (Epic, September 1987, No. 1 US / No. 1 UK) Bad / The Way You Make Me Feel / Speed Demon / Liberian Girl / Just Good Friends / Another Part of Me / Man in the Mirror / I Just Can't Stop Loving You / Dirty Diana / Smooth Criminal / Leave Me Alone

How on earth do you follow the album that had become the biggest selling of all time? The answer was simple: do the same thing but dress it in state-of-the-art sounds. Few albums sound more of their era than does *Bad*. However, it is a beautiful, bright pop record that contains arguably his greatest ballad ("I Just Can't Stop Loving You"), the unparalleled swagger of "The Way You Make Me Feel," and the anxious rock of "Smooth Criminal." One can only wonder what the title track would have sounded like if the original intention to duet with Prince had happened?

DANGEROUS (Epic, November 1991, No. 1 US / No. 1 US)
Jam / Why You Wanna Trip on Me / In the Closet / She Drives Me Wild / Remember the Time / Can't Let Her Get Away / Heal the World / Black or White / Who Is It / Give In to Me / Will You Be There / Keep the Faith/ Gone Too Soon / Dangerous

Jackson's first release without Quincy Jones since 1979, *Dangerous* was an ambitious, sprawling album that filled every second of the CD format's longer running time. Taking over a year to record it, Jackson worked with producer Teddy Riley for the R&B/new jack swing tracks, and Bill Bottrell for its rockier outings. *Dangerous* was arguably the last moment that Jackson was completely in step musically with the time. The ambitious "Jam" and "Black or White" still sound as fresh as when first heard, while the smooth sweetness of "Remember the Time" is one of Jackson's very best ballads. Following on from the 1985 single "We Are the World," "Heal the World" was another of Jackson's global anthems preaching harmony and unity.

HIStory: PAST, PRESENT, AND FUTURE, BOOK 1
(Epic, June 1995, No. 1 US / No. 1 UK)
Billie Jean / The Way You Make Me Feel / Black or White / Rock with You / She's Out of My Life / Bad / I Just Can't Stop Loving

You / Man in the Mirror / Thriller / Beat It / The Girl Is Mine / Remember the Time / Don't Stop 'til You Get Enough / Wanna Be Startin' Somethin' / Heal the World / Scream / They Don't Care About Us / Stranger in Moscow / This Time Around / Earth Song / D.S. / Money / Come Together / You Are Not Alone / Childhood / Tabloid Junkie / 2Bad / HIStory / Little Susie / Smile

Jackson's first release after the Jordan Chandler case, *HIStory* needed quickly to reconnect Michael Jackson with his fans and effortlessly reassert his superstardom. In the main, it did. A first disc of his greatest hits set the bar high for the disc of new material. Featuring a variety of producers, the highlights of second disc are many: "Scream," the Jam and Lewis-helmed industrial grind still sounds futuristic over two decades on; "You Are Not Alone" offers a tender moment; the crowd-dividing "Earth Song" became Jackson's biggest-selling UK hit of all-time. The album was not without controversy: the supposed anti-Semitism of "They Don't Care About Us" forced Jackson to change the song's lyrics.

BLOOD ON THE DANCE FLOOR: HIStory IN THE MIX (Epic, May 1997, No, 24 US / No. 1 UK)
Blood on the Dance Floor / Morphine / Superfly Sister / Ghosts / Is It Scary / Scream Louder (Flyte Tyme Remix) / Money (Fire Island Radio Edit) / 2Bad (Refugee Camp Mix) / Stranger in Moscow (Tee's In-House Club Mix) / This Time Around (D.M. Radio Mix) / Earth Song (Hani's Club Experience) / You Are Not Alone (Classic Club Mix) / HIStory (Tony Moran's History Lesson)

Following on from the half-new and half-old example of its parent album, *Blood on the Dance Floor: HIStory in the Mix* is possibly the most curious release in Jackson's catalogue. Appearing before eight of-their-moment and never less than enjoyable remixes of *HIStory* tracks, the five new songs were primarily conceived as the soundtrack to *Ghosts*, Jackson's latest short film. The tile track gave him anther UK No. 1 single, while "Morphine" is one of his strangest releases ever; the repeated use of "Demerol" in the chorus is a long way removed from "Rock with You."

INVINCIBLE (Epic, October 2001,
No. 1 US / No. 1 UK)
Unbreakable / Heartbreaker /
Invincible / Break of Dawn /
Heaven Can Wait / You Rock My
World / Butterflies / Speechless /
2000 Watts / You Are My Life /
Privacy / Don't Walk Away / Cry / The Lost Children / Whatever
Happens / Threatened

Released shortly after 9/11, Jackson's final studio album
of his lifetime was a somewhat underappreciated affair,
partially due to its length (seventy-seven minutes)
and the variety of producers involved (*ten* including
Jackson). There was a lot of material to get through
and it felt as if the world was moving on. Which was
a great shame as this is, outside of the obvious big-
hitters, one of the most interesting Jackson albums
to return to. Released in August 2001, "You Rock My
World" was the lead single; the highlights are the
opening "Unbreakable," which features a beyond-the-
grave rap from the Notorious B.I.G., and, deep within
the album, "Whatever Happens," which features an
expressive guitar solo from Carlos Santana.

MICHAEL (Epic, December
2010, No. 3 US / No. 4 UK)
Hold My Hand / Hollywood
Tonight / Keep Your Head Up /
I Like the Way You Love Me /
Monster / Best of Joy / Breaking
News / (I Can't Make It) Another
Day / Behind the Mask / Much
Too Soon

The inevitable posthumous opening of the MJ vault
began with these eight tracks. Largely recorded
between 2001 and his death, with most dating from
2007–2009, there was a feeling from many that these
songs had been released before their time and were
somewhat undercooked. The duet with Akon, "Hold
My Hand," was a poignant lead single, with its opening
line "This life don't live forever," yet although all the
component parts are there, it doesn't really sound like
a Michael Jackson record. Of greatest interest was the
oldest track, "Behind the Mask" which was originally
intended for *Thriller*, and shows to all the power that
Jackson had in full-flow.

XSCAPE (Epic, May 2014, No. 2
US / No. 1 UK)
Love Never Felt So Good / Chicago /
Loving You / A Place with No
Name / Slave to the Rhythm / Do
You Know Where Your Children
Are / Blue Gangsta / Xscape

There was to be little
of the controversy of Michael for *Xscape*, which
was overseen by L. A. Reid. It features material from
1983–1999, offering greater focus to Jackson's smoother
soulful side. Lead single "Love Never Felt So Good"
put him back in the US and UK Top 10. It was the
perfect opener: written with Paul Anka in 1983 and
subsequently recorded by Johnny Mathis, it is packed
with Jackson's *Thriller*-era tunefulness. "Loving You"
comes from the *Bad* era, while the later "A Place with
No Name" offers a wholly successful urban take on "A
Horse with No Name."

ENDNOTES

INTRODUCTION

1 www.oprah.com/oprahshow/Lisa-Marie-Pres-
leys-Blog-Post-About-Michael-Jackson#ixzz3wqrefHJo

2 news.bbc.co.uk/1/hi/entertainment/8137700.stm

3 www.oprah.com/oprahshow/Lisa-Marie-Presleys-Blog-Post-
About-Michael- Jackson#ixzz3wqrefHJo

4 www.rollingstone.com/music/news/read-madon
nas-vmas-speech-dedicated-to-michael-jackson-20090913#ix-
zz41NGJJxuj

CHAPTER 1

1 Jackson, Michael, and Bryan Monroe. "Michael Jackson in His
Own Words," Ebony magazine, Vol. 63, No. 2, December 2007.

2 www.businesswire.com/news/home/20080511005036/en

3 www.mjfancommunity.com/ebony.htm

4 George, Nelson. *Thriller: The Musical Life of Michael Jackson.*
(Cambridge: Da Capo Press, 2010), 207.

5 Langthorne, Mark, and Matt Richards. *83 Minutes: The Doctor,
the Damage, and the Shocking Death of Michael Jackson.* London: Blink Publishing, 2015.

6 Michael Jackson, *The Final Days*, CNN Special. www.youtube.
com/watch?v=rOY2hiXuLQw

7 www.cbs8.com/story/12681808/ap-timeline-details-michael-
jacksons-last-day

CHAPTER 2

1 Jackson, Michael, and Bryan Monroe. "Michael Jackson in His Own
Words," *Ebony* magazine, Vol. 63, No. 2, December 2007.

2 www.telegraph.co.uk/culture/music/michael-jack-
son/5704635/Former-manager-unveils-scale-of-Michael-Jack-
sons-drug-use.html

3 en.wikipedia.org/wiki/Trial_of_Michael_Jackson

4 www.rocksbackpages.com/Library/Article/michael-jackson-2

5 Grant, Adrian. *Michael Jackson: A Visual Documentary
1958–2009: The Official Tribute Edition.* (London: Omnibus
Press, 2009), 248.

6 Vogel, Joseph. *Man in the Music: The Creative Life and Work of
Michael Jackson.* (New York: Sterling, 2011), 251.

7 www.billboard.com/articles/news/58713/michael-jackson-
sails-with-two-seas

8 www.irishcentral.com/news/michael-jackson-planned-lepre-
chaun-theme-park-in-ireland-49183542-237648681.html

9 www.today.com/popculture/michael-jackson-making-music-
peas-1C9428439

10 speechismyhammer.com/features/will-i-am-hiphopdx/

11 George, Nelson. Thriller: The Musical Life of Michael Jackson.
(Cambridge: Da Capo Press, 2010), 207.

12 Jackson, Michael, and Bryan Monroe. "Michael Jackson in His
Own Words," Ebony magazine, Vol. 63, No. 2, December 2007.

CHAPTER 3

1 www.getmusic.com October 26, 2001

2 www.mtv.com/news/1442947/carlos-santana-re-cords-with-michael-jackson/

3 Vogel, Joseph. *Man in the Music: The Creative Life and Work of Michael Jackson*. (New York: Sterling, 2011), 222.

4 Beaumont, Mark. www.nme.com/reviews/michael-jack-son/5780#XjTHFez65kzlhqUi.99

5 Murray, Scott. www.theguardian.com/music/2009/jun/26/michael-jackson-exeter-city-geller

6 news.bbc.co.uk/1/hi/entertainment/2088831.stm

7 Grant, Adrian. *Michael Jackson: A Visual Documentary 1958–2009: The Official Tribute Edition.* (London: Omni-bus Press, 2009), 230.

CHAPTER 4

1 Bronson, Fred. *The Billboard Book of Number One Hits*, updated and expanded, 5th ed. (New York: Billboard Books, 2003), 839.

2 www.youtube.com/watch?v=JGOXe_w7ykI

3 Easlea, Daryl. www.rocksbackpages.com/Library/Ar-ticle/dont-stop-til-you-get-enough-bruce-swedien-re-members-the-times-with-michael-jackson

4 Weinraub, Bernard. www.nytimes.com/1995/06/15/arts/in-new-lyrics-jackson-uses-slurs.html

5 metro.co.uk/2016/02/19/its-been-20-years-since-jarvis-cockers-bare-bum-invaded-michael-jacksons-perfor-mance-at-the-brits-5705787/

6 www.youtube.com/watch?v=eK0Ynq9Kl1k

7 Taraborrelli, J. Randy. *Michael Jackson: The Magic and the Madness.* (London: Sidgwick & Jackson, 2003), 582.

8 Ibid., 590.

9 www.rocksbackpages.com/Library/Article/the-starman-who-fell-to-earth-michael-jackson-don-valley-stadium-sheffield-

10 www.rocksbackpages.com/Library/Article/michael-jack-son--blood-on-the-dance-floor

11 Ibid.

CHAPTER 5

1 Taraborrelli, J. Randy. *Michael Jackson: The Magic and the Madness.* (London: Sidgwick & Jackson, 2003), 450.

2 Ibid., 464.

3 ibid., 478.

4 George, Nelson. *Thriller: The Musical Life of Michael Jack-son.* (Cambridge: Da Capo Press, 2010), 206.

5 Taraborrelli, J. Randy. *Michael Jackson: The Magic and the Madness.* (London: Sidgwick & Jackson, 2003), 538.

6 Ibid., 544.

7 Johnson, Robert E. "Michael Tells 'Where I Met Lisa Marie And How I Proposed.' " Ebony magazine, October 1994, p. 119.

8 www.oprah.com/oprahshow/Lisa-Marie-Pres-leys-Blog-Post-About-Michael-Jackson#ixzz3wqrefHJo

CHAPTER 6

1 www.rocksbackpages.com/Library/Article/michael-jack-son-idangerous

2 Yetnikoff, Walter, with David Ritz. *Howling at the Moon: Confessions of a Music Mogul in an Age of Excess.* (Lon-don: Abacus, 2004), 161.

3 Sullivan, Caroline. www.theguardian.com/music/2009/jun/26/michael-jackson-obituary

4 Graves, Tom. Michael Jackson/1987/Tom Graves/Rock & Roll Disc/Michael Jackson: Bad. www.rocksbackpages.com/Library/Article/michael-jacksoni-badi

5 Bronson, Fred. *The Billboard Book of Number One Hits*, updated and expanded, 5th ed. (New York: Billboard Books, 2003), 702.

6 George, Nelson. *Thriller: The Musical Life of Michael Jack-son.* (Cambridge: Da Capo Press, 2010), 190–91.

7 Snow, Mat. www.rocksbackpages.com/Library/Article/michael-jackson-idangerous

8 George, Nelson. *Thriller: The Musical Life of Michael Jack-son.* (Cambridge: Da Capo Press, 2010), 196.

9 Easlea, Daryl. www.rocksbackpages.com/Library/Ar-ticle/dont-stop-til-you-get-enough-bruce-swedien-re-members-the-times-with-michael-jackson

5   Yetnikoff, Walter, with David Ritz. *Howling at the Moon: Confessions of a Music Mogul in an Age of Excess*. (London: Abacus, 2004), 90.

6   Jackson, Michael. *Moonwalk*. (London: Heinemann, 2009), 111.

7   Grant, Adrian. *Michael Jackson: A Visual Documentary 1958–2009: The Official Tribute Edition*. (London: Omnibus Press, 2009), 30.

8   Neal, Mark Anthony. *Michael Jackson: Hello World: The Motown Solo Collection*. (Los Angeles: Hip-O Select, 2009), 17.

9   Yetnikoff, Walter, with David Ritz. *Howling at the Moon: Confessions of a Music Mogul in an Age of Excess*. (London: Abacus, 2004), 90.

10 Taraborrelli, J. Randy. *Michael Jackson: The Magic and the Madness*. (London: Sidgwick & Jackson, 2003), 137–47.

11 Jackson, Michael, and Bryan Monroe. "Michael Jackson in His Own Words," Ebony magazine, Vol. 63, No. 2, December 2007.

CHAPTER 14

1   Brackett, David (ed.). *The Pop, Rock and Soul Reader: Histories and Debates*, 3rd ed. (New York: Oxford University Press, 2014), 174.

2   Ibid.

3   Ales, Barney, and Adam White. *Motown: The Sound of Young America*. (New York: Thames & Hudson, 2016), 258.

4   Taraborrelli, J. Randy. *Michael Jackson: The Magic and the Madness*. (London: Sidgwick & Jackson, 2003), 49.

5   Jackson, Michael. *Moonwalk*. (London: Heinemann, 2009), 68.

6   Taraborrelli, J. Randy. *Michael Jackson: The Magic and the Madness*. (London: Sidgwick & Jackson, 2003), 58.

7   George, Nelson. *The Michael Jackson Story*. (London: New English Library, 1984), 42.

8   Easlea, Daryl www.bbc.co.uk/music/reviews/8c9p

9   Jackson, Michael. *Moonwalk*. (London: Heinemann, 2009), 86.

10 George, Nelson. *The Michael Jackson Story*. (London: New English Library, 1984), 44.

11 Bronson, Fred, and Adam White. *The Billboard Book of Number One Rhythm and Blues Hits*. (New York: Billboard Books, 1993), 410.

CHAPTER 15

1   Jackson, Michael, and Bryan Monroe. "Michael Jackson in His Own Words," Ebony magazine, Vol. 63, No. 2, December 2007.

2   Taraborrelli, J. Randy. *Michael Jackson: The Magic and the Madness*. (London: Sidgwick & Jackson, 2003), 19.

3   George, Nelson. *The Michael Jackson Story*. (London: New English Library, 1984), 19.

4   Jackson, Michael. *Moonwalk*. (London: Heinemann, 2009), 24.

5 Ibid., 32.

6 Ibid., 34.

7 Ibid., 43.

AFTERWORD

1   Jackson, Michael, and Bryan Monroe. "Michael Jackson in His Own Words," Ebony magazine, Vol. 63, No. 2, December 2007.

2   Pulver, Andrew. www.theguardian.com/music/2009/oct/28/michael-jackson-this-is-it-review

3   Ibid.

4   Vogel, Joseph. *Man in the Music: The Creative Life and Work of Michael Jackson*. (New York: Sterling, 2011), 253

5   www.bbc.co.uk/news/world-us-canada-24375844

6   www.forbes.com/pictures/gjdm45jmj/michael-jackson-contd

7   Easlea, Daryl. www.rocksbackpages.com/Library/Article/dont-stop-til-you-get-enough-bruce-swedien-remembers-the-times-with-michael-jackson

PHOTO CREDITS

CHAPTER 4: I AM HERE WITH YOU

p. 34: © Kevin Mazur/WireImage/Getty Images

p. 36: © Brian Harris /The Independent/REX/Shutterstock

p. 37 (bottom): © Liaison/Hulton Archive/Getty Images

p. 38: © Larry Busacca/WireImage/Getty Images

p. 39: © Jeff Kravitz/FilmMagic/Getty Images

p. 40: © Kevin Mazur/WireImage/Getty Images

p. 41: © Bruce Bailey/REX/Shutterstock

pp. 42–43: © Times Newspapers Ltd/REX/Shutterstock

p. 43: © Photoshot/Getty Images

p. 44: © Dave Benett/Getty Images

p. 47: © Laurens van Houten/Frank White Photo Agency

pp. 48–49: © Mahesh Bhat/Hulton Archive/Getty Images

CHAPTER 5: TALKIN', SQUEALIN', LYIN'?

p. 50: © Georges De Keerle/Getty Images

p. 53: © Nikos Vinieratos/REX/Shutterstock

p. 54: © Stewart Cook/REX/Shutterstock

p. 55: © Leon Schadeberg/REX/Shutterstock

p. 56: © Randy Bauer/REX/Shutterstock

p. 57 (top): © Yvonne Hemsey/Getty Images; (bottom):
   © Mark Reinstein/REX/Shutterstock

p. 59: © Pool ARNAL/PAT/Gamma-Rapho/Getty Images

p. 60: © Jeff Kravitz/FilmMagic/Getty Images

CHAPTER 6: I AM TIRED OF THIS BUSINESS

p. 62: © Ron Galella/WireImage

p. 65: © Gary Lewis/mptvimages.com

p. 66: © Raymond Boyd/Getty Images

p. 67: © L. Cohen/WireImage/Getty Images

p. 69: © Peter Still/Redferns/Getty Images

pp. 70, 71: © Laurens van Houten/Frank White Photo Agency

p. 72: © Damian Strohmeyer /Sports Illustrated/Getty Images

p. 73 (top): © L. Cohen/WireImage/Getty Images; (bottom):
   © Chris Wilkins/AFP/Getty Images

p. 74: © Ron Galella/WireImage/Getty Images

p. 75: © The LIFE Picture Collection/Getty Images

CHAPTER 7: THE WHOLE WORLD HAS TO ANSWER RIGHT NOW

p. 76: © Steve Douglass/Associated Newspapers /REX/Shutterstock

p. 78 (top): © John D. Kisch/Separate Cinema Archive/Getty

Images; (bottom): © Afro American Newspapers/Gado/
Getty Images

p. 79: © John D. Kisch/Separate Cinema Archive/Getty Images

p. 80: © Sankei Archive/Getty Images

p. 82: © Afro American Newspapers/Gado/Getty Images

p. 84: © Dave Hogan/Hulton Archive/Getty Images

p. 85: © Peter Still/Redferns/Getty Images

p. 86 (top): © Ian Parry/Associated Newspapers /REX/Shutterstock;
   (bottom): © IPC MAGAZINES: CHAT/REX/Shutterstock

p. 87: © Frank White Photo Agency

p. 88: © Vinnie Zuffante/Hulton Archive/Getty Images

p. 89: © L. Busacca/WireImage/Getty Images

pp. 90, 91: © Moviestore Collection/REX/Shutterstock

pp. 92–93: © Michael Ochs Archives/Getty Images

CHAPTER 8: YOU GOT ME SUPERSONIC, BABY

p. 94: © Georges De Keerle/Getty Images

p. 95: © Moviestore Collection/REX/Shutterstock

p. 98: © Bettmann/Getty Images

p. 99: © Walter McBride/Corbis/Getty Images

p. 100: © Dean Messina/Frank White Photo Agency

p. 101: © Ron Galella/WireImage/Getty Images

p. 102: © Dennis Stone/REX/Shutterstock

pp. 103 (top and bottom), 104–105: © Dean Messina/Frank White
   Photo Agency

p. 107 (top): © Ron Galella/WireImage/Getty Images; (bottom):
   © Hulton Archive/Getty Images

p. 109: © Daily Mail /REX/Shutterstock

CHAPTER 9: NO MERE MORTAL CAN RESIST

p. 110: © Eugene Adebari/REX/Shutterstock

p. 112: © Gabi Rona/mptvimages.com

p. 113: © Ron Galella/WireImage/Getty Images

p. 114: © Bobby Holland/mptvimages.com

p. 115, top: © Astrid Stawiarz/Getty Images

p. 116: © Chris Walter/WireImage/Getty Images

pp. 118, 119: © Paul Drinkwater/NBC/NBCU Photo Bank/Getty Images

pp. 122–123: © Afro American Newspapers/Gado/Getty Images

CHAPTER 10: THE STARS DO SHINE

p. 124: © Andre Csillag/REX/Shutterstock

p. 126: © Lynne McAfee/REX/Shutterstock

INDEX

Page references in *italics* indicate photographs.

ACKNOWLEDGMENTS

I would like to thank Ndugu Chancler for his time and for playing some of the most memorable drum parts in history, and all family, friends, and the team at Quarto for their remarkable support.

ABOUT THE AUTHOR

© Keith Hammond

Writer, DJ, and broadcaster Daryl Easlea's books explore his favorite loves: great pop eccentrics, populist African-American music, and prog rock. His extended essay, *The Story of the Supremes*, accompanied the V&A exhibition of the same name in 2008. He believes that "Don't Stop 'til You Get Enough" is one of the top 5 records ever made.